Exploring Xenakis

Performance, Practice, Philosophy

Edited by
Alfia Nakipbekova
University of Leeds, UK

Series in Music

VERNON PRESS

Copyright © 2020 Vernon Press, an imprint of Vernon Art and Science Inc, on behalf of the author.

All rights reserved. No part of this publication may be reproduced, stored in a retrieval system, or transmitted in any form or by any means, electronic, mechanical, photocopying, recording, or otherwise, without the prior permission of Vernon Art and Science Inc.

www.vernonpress.com

In the Americas:
Vernon Press
1000 N West Street,
Suite 1200, Wilmington,
Delaware 19801
United States

In the rest of the world:
Vernon Press
C/Sancti Espiritu 17,
Malaga, 29006
Spain

Series in Music

Library of Congress Control Number: 2019931087

ISBN: 978-1-62273-792-5

Also available: 978-1-62273-323-1 [Hardback]; 978-1-62273-657-7 [PDF, E-Book]

Cover design by Vernon Press.

Cover image: Photo of Iannis Xenakis courtesy of Mâkhi Xenakis.

Product and company names mentioned in this work are the trademarks of their respective owners. While every care has been taken in preparing this work, neither the authors nor Vernon Art and Science Inc. may be held responsible for any loss or damage caused or alleged to be caused directly or indirectly by the information contained in it.

Every effort has been made to trace all copyright holders, but if any have been inadvertently overlooked the publisher will be pleased to include any necessary credits in any subsequent reprint or edition.

Table of contents

	Introduction	*v*
	Alfia Nakipbekova	
	Part I - Xenakis and the avant-garde	*1*
Chapter 1	**'Xenakis, not Gounod': Xenakis, the avant garde, and May '68**	3
	Alannah Marie Halay and Michael D. Atkinson	
	Part II - Compositional practice	*19*
Chapter 2	**The Berlin sketches and Xenakis's middle-period style**	21
	Dimitris Exarchos	
Chapter 3	**Stratification of sound masses in Xenakis's *Gmeeoorh* (1974)**	37
	Marina Sudo	
Chapter 4	**On *Herma***	53
	Benoît Gibson	
	Part III - Performance	*67*
Chapter 5	**Performances in Iannis Xenakis's electroacoustic music**	69
	Reinhold Friedl	
Chapter 6	**Performing *Nomos alpha* by Iannis Xenakis: reflections on interpretative space**	89
	Alfia Nakipbekova	
Chapter 7	***Nomos alpha*. Remarks on performance**	109
	Makis Solomos	
	Index	*129*

Introduction

Alfia Nakipbekova

Iannis Xenakis (1922-2001) is universally recognised as one of the most significant and influential musicians of the twentieth century. His artistic output and its enormous impact on musical philosophy, compositional methods, sound and instrumental techniques has drawn considerable attention from numerous researchers and an array of committed performers, whose work interweaves and cross-pollinates within the multiple spectra of the richly patterned fabric of Xenakis's universe.

Xenakian studies have been developing since the mid-1960s consisting of multi-faceted contributions and approaches expounded in monographs, journal articles and PhD dissertations;[1] this field is continuing to expand with new theoretical insights and practical experiences from a diverse community of international musicologists, mathematicians, philosophers and performers.[2] Integral to this growth, the gatherings of dedicated researchers at conferences and symposia devoted to Xenakis's legacy play an important role as the dynamic junctures within this momentum. Such opportunities to

---

[1] As noted by the editor Makis Solomos in the Introduction to *Présences de/Presences of Iannis Xenakis*. 2001, 3. Paris: Centre de documentation de la musique contemporaine. For the complete annotated bibliographies compiled and commented by Makis Solomos, see the appendix of *Présences de/Presences of Iannis Xenakis*, and 'The Friends of Iannis Xenakis Association', online http://www.iannis-xenakis.org/xen/read/biblio.html

[2] Recent studies have included: *Iannis Xenakis, La musique électroacoustique / The Electroacoustic Music, Musique-philosophie*. 2015, edited by Makis Solomos. Paris: L'Harmattan; Margarethe Maierhofer-Lischka, 2017. 'Approaching the Liminal in the Performance of Iannis Xenakis' Instrumental Solo Works'. *ÍMPAR Journal for Artistic Research*, 1(2): 45-53; J. Janković-Beguš, 2016. 'Playing the Game with Aleatorics and Narrativity: Linaia-Agon by Iannis Xenakis.' *New Sound, International Journal of Music*, 48 (2): 109-130; Maia Sigua, 2016. 'Oresteia by Iannis Xenakis: A New Solution to a 400-Year-Old Problem'. In *Music on Stage* 2, edited by Luis Campos and Fiona Jane Schopf. Cambridge Scholars Publishing; Christian Utz, 2016. 'Time-Space Experience in Works for Solo Cello by Lachenmann, Xenakis and Ferneyhough: a Performance-Sensitive Approach to Morphosyntactic Musical Analysis'. *Music Analysis*, 36 (2): 216-256. https://onlineli brary.wiley.com/doi/10.1111/musa.12076

discuss and evaluate the latest findings and projects-in-progress render long-term ramifications.

One of the most significant publications reflecting this important part in Xenakian studies is the book *Présences de/Presences of Iannis Xenakis* (2001) comprised of the proceedings of the first ever symposium devoted solely to Xenakis, 'Presences of Iannis Xenakis'.[3] The research papers from the two consequential events that followed – 'Symposium Iannis Xenakis', Athens, May 2005 and 'Xenakis International Symposium', London, April, 2011 – are also available.[4] The range of the topics and approaches in these publications is astonishingly broad and vibrant: from theoretical analyses to increasingly diverging philosophical, aesthetical and interdisciplinary paths towards the heart of Xenakis's creative source. Makis Solomos' words, written almost two decades ago, are still relevant today:

> "The time has come to rectify (while not necessarily erasing) the image that continues to dominate: the image of a composer-"mathematician". Xenakis has defined himself only as a "user of mathematics" [...] His music itself is far from generalizing any formalization." (*Présences de/Presences of Iannis Xenakis*, 2001, 4)

Continuing the tradition of sharing manifold theoretical and practical perspectives and paths in Xenakian studies, this book consists of selected papers presented at the Symposium 'Exploring Xenakis: Performance, Practice, Philosophy' (Leeds, 2017).[5] The one-day Symposium brought together scholars from the UK, France, Japan, Australia, Belgium, Portugal, the Netherlands and Brazil. Compared to the Symposium proceedings mentioned above, the scope of this book is circumscribed by the scale of the event; the resulting articles, however, reflect a variety of research questions encompassing Xenakis's compositional methods, reflections on performance, and the composer's ideological position with regard to the avant-garde. The

---

[3] The Symposium took place on 29-30 January 1998 at the Centre de Documentation de la Musique Contemporaine (CDMC) and Radio France, Paris.

[4] *International Symposium Iannis Xenakis: conference proceedings: Athens 18-20 May 2005 Greece,* edited by Anastasia Georgaki and Makis Solomos. Panepistēmio Athēnōn [Athens]: National and Kapodistrian University of Athens, 2005; *Xenakis Programme Details,* Goldsmith, University of London, 2011, edited by Dimitris Exarchos. Online https://www.gold.ac.uk/cmru/xenakis-international-symposium/programme/

[5] The Symposium took place on 12 September 2017 at the School of Music, University of Leeds, supported by the RAM (the Royal Musical Association). The keynote lectures were given by Dr. Makis Solomos and Dr. Benoît Gibson.

Introduction vii

chapters are arranged in three parts: 'Xenakis and the avant-garde', 'Compositional practice', and 'Performance'. The main works examined here are *Metastaseis* (1953-54), *Gmeeoorh* (1974), *Herma* (1961), *Légende d'Eer* (1978), *Bohor* (1962) and *Nomos alpha* (1966).

In Part I, Xenakis's relationship with the avant-garde is explored – Alannah Marie Halay and Michael D. Atkinson investigate the significance of Xenakis's creative force in the rumbustious atmosphere of Paris in May 1968, elucidating 'how Xenakis and those like him became central to the revolutionary consciousness of the day, and what it is about Xenakis's practice that paradoxically disavows such possibilities.' (See chapter one, p. 3).

In Atkinson's words, 'Xenakis's work is placed in the context of its reception and 'canonicity' today, and questions whether such instantiation and acceptance manages to undermine that which was once so 'active'.'

In Part II, various aspects of Xenakis's compositional style and technique are discussed – some of the mathematical procedures employed in his works and the resulting sonorities and textures, as well as the processes involved in the composer's search for authentic expression. Part II opens with the chapter that focuses on Xenakis's middle-period style (1961-1973) from the perspective of Xenakis's compositional development. Dimitris Exarchos examines sketches and hand-written calculations made in the early 1960s in Berlin, when the composer was searching and refining his philosophical concepts and compositional techniques; this significant juncture is denoted by the composer's discovery of the outside-time structures that enabled him to develop a generalised metatheory of composition. The focus of this chapter is the genesis of these ideas on the mathematical level and their musical applications in the following decades (although the author also re-interprets Xenakis's earlier work accordingly). Taking as the case study the only work composed by Xenakis for organ, *Gmeeoorh* (1974), Marina Sudo scrutinises the factors that determine the degree and quality of densities and complexities of sound masses created by using 'a variety of timbres in combination with textural writing based upon linear arborescences'. (See chapter three, p. 39). As defined by Sudo, the paper 'aims to describe the structure of the different levels of sound mass, focusing on the following questions: which factors determine the quality of each sonic event, how do they interact, and how are the different types of cluster stratified? In addition to the analysis of the published score, an aural analysis of recordings of *Gmeeoorh*, informed by the *spectromorphological* approach originally derived from Schaeffer's concept of "l'écoute réduite [reductive listening]", is presented.' In chapter four 'On *Herma*', Benoît Gibson offers new insights into the structure and sound of this early work for piano and relationship between *Herma* and one of the earlier pieces *Achorripsis* (1957). A wide range of questions is examined – from compositional concerns, such as classes of pitches, structure, graphic representation and stochastic distribution, to the problematic of editions and recording. Gibson includes a detailed overview of the commercially issued recordings of *Herma*, comparing and discussing the issues of the interpretative approaches in some of the recordings. The notion of *precision* in realisation of *Herma* is relevant to other instrumentalists, as each interpreter must confront the task of achieving a distinctive balance of the elements (pitches, densities, dynamics, etc.) within the complexity of a particular Xenakis's composition.

The subject of performing Xenakis's music is richly illuminated in *Performing Xenakis* (2010),[6] an important publication that draws together the experiences and reflections on interpretation and techniques directly from distinguished performers. In Part III of this book, the authors approach the performative aspect in Xenakis's music from three singular perspectives: as a 'secret' element in some of Xenakis's electroacoustic compositions; the interdisciplinary exploration of the sonority, structure and cinematic allusions (with reference to the Russian cinematographer Andrei Tarkovsky's film *Stalker*, 1979) evoked through the process of internalising *Nomos alpha*; and the exploration of the possible interpretative and technical solutions involved in performing and recording of the piece – one of the most complex and rewarding compositions for solo cello – demonstrated through analysing and comparing the selected recordings. In chapter five, Reinhold Friedl examines the rarely mentioned hidden performative aspects of Xenakis's electroacoustic music: not the performance *of* his electroacoustic music but the performances *for* his electroacoustic music. His detailed exposition of the recorded material and its background re-emphasises the uniqueness of Xenakian textures. By examining the recordings of *La Légende d'Eer* (1978) and *Bohor* (1962), Friedl argues the possibility of the unnamed performers being involved in creating the body of intermeshed electronic and live sound. *Nomos alpha* is the focus of the following two chapters. Chapter six conveys cellist Alfia Nakipbekova's personal experience of mastering *Nomos alpha*. (To listen to the recording of *Nomos alpha* by Alfia Nakipbekova see link https://soundcloud.com/alfianakipbekova/iannis-xenakis-nomos-alpha). Although the work has been thoroughly analysed in terms of Xenakis's use of mathematical procedures in organising the compositional material, a close exploration of the work's interdisciplinary and philosophical aspects from the performer's subjective viewpoint (termed as the Associative Method), has not been previously undertaken. As outlined in the

---

[6] *Performing Xenakis*, 2010. Translated, compiled and edited by Sharon Kanach. Hillsdale, New York: Pendragon Press.

chapter, the arduous process of striving to unravel the essence of Xenakian expression while engaging with the challenges of the new physicality, engenders the moments of insights, a recurring state of clarity in which the composition is perceived as a 'window', the opening toward the expanses of the totality of Xenakian musical megacosm. At these moments, *Nomos alpha* is transformed from the singularity of a 'difficult' piece for cello into a catalyst for reaching new knowledge in the realm of expression and philosophy of performance. In chapter seven, Makis Solomos considers the subject of performance in recorded versions of *Nomos alpha* 'which has still been little investigated', (See chapter seven, p. 110) tracing the development of the work's performance tradition over three generations of cellists: from Siegfried Palm (who premiered the piece), Pierre Penassou and Rohan de Saram, to the 'second generation' – Pierre Strauch, Christophe Roy and Arne Deforce; among the 'third generation' of *Nomos alpha* cellists he includes Martina Schucan, Moritz Müllenbach and Alfia Nakipbekova. Solomos' close perusal of the recordings of *Nomos alpha* by Roy and Deforce reveals the potentialities in developing the interpretative space through comparing the two versions from 'specifically Xenakian aspects', such as 'sound, energy, gestuality', identifying these two approaches to interpretation as *chthonic* and *cosmic*. The chapter includes excerpts from Solomos' interviews with the two musicians – these lively discussions generate as many questions as they offer personal insights and practical experiences by the performers.

This chapter, dedicated to the evaluation of conceptual and expressive depths confronting the interpreters of Xenakis's music, concludes the book as an invitation to further research in the developing performance practice area within the fertile terrain of Xenakis's music – the source of bountiful vitality and potential for limitless proliferation across disciplines, cultures and paths to knowledge.

References

Présences de/Presences of Iannis Xenakis. 2001, edited by Makis Solomos. Paris, Centre de documentation de la musique contemporaine.

Acknowledgements

I wish to thank the School of Music, University of Leeds and the RMA (Royal Musical Association), especially Dr. Michael Spencer for his support and contribution to the Symposium, Prof. Michael Allis for his valuable advice on the manuscript, Susan Bagust and Michael Byde (RMA) for their help in organising the event; Dr. Makis Solomos and Dr. Benoît Gibson for their keynote lectures and support for the project, the participants of the Symposium and the contributors to this publication: Michael D. Atkinson, Said Athié Bonduki (University of São Paulo, Brazil), Dr. Dimitris Exarchos

(Goldsmiths, University of London), Reinhold Friedl (Goldsmiths, University of London), Dr. Benoît Gibson (University of Évora), Dr. Alannah Halay (University of Leeds), Nikos Ioakeim (independent researcher), Dr. Yuko Ohara (Senzoku Gakuen College of Music, Japan), Marlēnē Radice (Sir Zelman Cowan School of Music, Monash University), Prof. Makis Solomos (Université Paris 8), Marina Sudo, University of Leuven.

Special thanks to Mâkhi Xenakis for her kind permission to use the photo of Iannis Xenakis, Pierre Carré (Xenakis Archives), Dr. Ewan Stefani and CePRA (Centre for Practice-Led Research in the Arts), University of Leeds.

Biographies

Dr. Alannah Marie Halay (AFHEA) is an academic researcher, composer and sound artist. After completing her PhD (*Recognising Absurdity through Compositional Practice: Comparing an Avant-Garde Style with being avant garde*) in 2016, she worked as a Research Fellow in the Leeds Humanities Research Institute, and a visiting lecturer at the University of Leeds. As well as performing her own music as a multi-instrumentalist and improviser, her music has been performed in Denmark, England, the Netherlands, and Poland; in events such as the Gaudeamus Muziekweek Festival and the 'Leeds Lieder+' song festival; by ensembles such as Notes Inégales, Trio Layers, Bloomsbury Opera, percussion ensembles of the Musikhochschule Freiburg and the University of Leeds, the Yorkshire Young Sinfonia, and others. She was the first winner of the Yorkshire Young Sinfonia Composition Competition in 2015, and her music has been selected for the Gaudeamus Muziekweek Academy. Most recently, she collaborated with the School of Music at the University of Leeds on a composition for 28 Steinway pianos. The project celebrated the School of Music becoming a Steinway School. Alannah is also the founder and organiser of the international *(Per)Forming Art* Symposium. She is also editor and co-author of the book *(Per)Forming Art: Performance as Research in Contemporary Artworks*. Alannah has also worked as a journalist, having written articles about conferences and music festivals for the Royal Musical Association and *Sounds Like Now: Contemporary Music News*.

Michael Atkinson is a critical theorist from Rochdale, England. He studied for his English degree at Sheffield Hallam University, receiving a First Class Honours, before graduating with the same for his Master's degree in Critical & Cultural Theory from the University of Leeds. His work has been published by Cambridge Scholars Publishing and WRoCaH amongst others. In addition to theory, Michael takes part in performance art, having performed in several Slam Poetry events during his time at Sheffield University. With a particular interest in

Introduction xi

dialectics and Western Marxism, Mike follows the teachings of a wide array of thinkers, and has written on topics as diverse as the Uncanny, the 'absurd', *Oliver Twist*, *Doctor Who*, the commodification of nostalgia, and the anxiety and sense of guilt experienced by those of us who aren't engaged in manual labour.

Dr. Dimitris Exarchos is a theorist and musicologist specializing in contemporary music. He has published in books and journals on twentieth-century composition, theory, and analysis. He has delivered talks in the UK and abroad, organised symposia (Xenakis International Symposium; Notation in Contemporary Music; Compositional Aesthetics and the Political) and curated concerts and events (Southbank Centre, Goldsmiths, Migrant Sound). His research explores the themes of temporality, notation, and materialism, on the intersections between philosophy, aesthetics, analysis, and composition; his analytical work includes computational and mathematical approaches. He is currently Visiting Research Fellow at the Contemporary Music Research Unit, Goldsmiths.

Marina Sudo completed her first degree and master's in musicology at the Tokyo University of the Arts. In 2015, supported by the award of a stipend by the Paul Sacher Foundation, Basel, she conducted a study of the manuscript sketches and scores held in their Pierre Boulez collection. She is currently a PhD student in musicology at the University of Leuven. In her PhD project, she seeks to explore the constructive potential of 'noise' in contemporary musical practice, the analytical focus being on works by Xenakis, Lachenmann, Ablinger and Merzbow.

Dr. Benoît Gibson studied viola, musical analysis and music theory at the Conservatoire de Musique de Montreal in Canada. He then moved to Paris (France) where he completed his PhD on the music of Iannis Xenakis at the École de hautes études en sciences sociales. Between 2000 and 2007, he worked at the Lisbon School of Music (Escola Superior de Música de Lisboa) in Portugal. He is presently teaching musical analysis at the University of Évora (Portugal) where, between 2008 and 2014, he directed the Centre for Research in Music and Musicology (Unidade de Investigação em Música e Musicologia – UnIMeM). During that period, he also worked on the critical edition of Iannis Xenakis's writings in collaboration with Makis Solomos and Sharon Kanach. The publication of his book *The Instrumental Music of Iannis Xenakis. Theory, Practice, Self-Borrowing* (2011) has been widely recognised as a major contribution to the understanding of the composer's creative thinking.

Reinhold Friedl studied mathematics in Stuttgart and Berlin, piano with Renate Werner, Alan Marks and Alexander von Schlippenbach, composition with Mario Bertoncini and Witold Szalonek. Reinhold is a composer and performer, director of the ensemble Zeitkratzer. He has received commissions from Wiener Festwochen, BBC London, the French state, Berliner Festspiele, ZKM, etc., and has written numerous articles and radio features on electronic music, notably for WDR Studio elektronische Musik Cologne. Reinhold lectures and teaches at the University Paris 8, Berlin UdK, London Goldsmiths University, Musikhochschule Basel, Music University Thessaloniki, a.o. He is currently completing a PhD on Iannis Xenakis's electroacoutic music at Goldsmiths, University of London.

Alfia Nakipbekova is an internationally acclaimed soloist and pedagogue. She studied cello with Mstislav Rostropovich, Daniil Shafran and Jacqueline du Pré. She is a recipient of the Special Prize for Outstanding Mastery of the Cello at the Casals Competition in Budapest. Alfia studied Comparative Literature and Cultural Studies at Birkbeck, University of London, where she received the Marjorie Gould Prize and the Dean's Award. Alfia teaches at Leeds Conservatoire, University of Leeds and the Guildhall School of Music and Drama, London. She is currently researching the development of the cello in the late twentieth century for her PhD thesis *Performing Contemporary Cello Music: Defining the Interpretative Space* at the University of Leeds, and has given presentations and lecture-recitals performing *Nomos alpha* by Iannis Xenakis at various conferences, including Radboud University Nijmegen (Deleuze & Aesthetics); Universities of Birmingham, Bangor, York, Leeds, Hong Kong and Rome (Deleuze Studies Conference); University Paris 8, Goldsmiths, University of London, the Guildhall School of Music and Drama, and Norwegian Academy of Music, Oslo (Performance Studies Network Conference 2018). In September 2017 Alfia organised Symposium 'Exploring Xenakis: Performance, Practice, Philosophy', supported by the RMA and School of Music, University of Leeds.

Prof. Makis Solomos was born in Athens in 1962 and studied composition and musicology in Paris. From 1998 to 2010, he was an associate professor at University Montpellier 3. Since 2010, he is Professor at University Paris 8. He is the director of the research team MUSIDANSE. As a musicologist, he has published numerous books, articles, and papers. He also organised many symposiums and edited their proceedings. His research belongs to two main fields:

> 1. Research on Xenakis. One of the leading figures in Xenakis studies, he has opened new paths in this field. In his first

works, "bracketing" (in the phenomenological sense of the word) Xenakis's music, he showed that it could be analysed as composed sound. Then he investigated the world of the young Xenakis (before *Metastaseis*). After the opening of Xenakis's archives following the composer's death in 2001, he began to work on the critical edition of his writings. He started conducting genetic studies with instrumental as well as electroacoustic music. His last project is about performing Xenakis's music.

2. Research on today's music and art. He explored various subjects: the question of space, the relationship between technics and technology, the notion of globalization, spectral music, the granular paradigm... In his book *De la musique au son. L'émergence du son dans la musique des XXe-XXIe siècles* (English translation forthcoming), he examines how sound has become a major issue for music. His recent researches are about the idea of ecology of sound in the broad sense. He is working on the project 'Arts, ecologies, translations', preparing a book on the subject.

Part I -
Xenakis and the avant-garde

Chapter 1

'Xenakis, not Gounod':
Xenakis, the avant garde, and May '68

Alannah Marie Halay and Michael D. Atkinson

It is perhaps odd to centre a text around a connection whose principal evidence seems to be, at first glance, nothing more than sloganeering. The relationships between Iannis Xenakis and the events and spirit of the protests of May 1968 are, however, manifold, if rather obscure. It is the intent of this piece to explore these relationships and what they infer. Several detours will need to be made to eke them out, to demonstrate their veracity, tenuous, as they may seem. The demonstration of such a link provides a useful way of framing and exploring the work of the composer, as well as providing an elucidation of the aesthetic and political desires of those involved in the protests.

Throughout this text, we will attempt to demonstrate how theory (and by extension research) and praxis/practice are not to be considered as absolute opposites, rather, we endeavour to show how the two mediate one another. We will also attempt to demonstrate how practice, which inevitably encompasses a theoretical component, also encompasses a certain political 'approach', or ideology. The aim of this essay is, therefore, to explore the ways in which, consciously or unconsciously, the work of Xenakis aided the 'ethos' behind May '68 and events like it by opening up a space of freedom for musical and aesthetic exploration. The reason why Xenakis is such a useful object of study for what is an attempt to understand the relationship between the 'avant garde' and apparently revolutionary politics is that, apart from aesthetic possibilities (or lack thereof), the participants of May '68 drew a direct link between their activities and the composer: one of the examples of the graffiti to be found in Paris was 'Xenakis, not Gounod' (Harley 2005, 64).

From the informed bravado of the Situationist International in their critique of the totality of capitalism and its inherent boredom and alienation (the alienation between people, between workers and their object of labour, between inhabitants and the city they inhabit) to oblique statements of aesthetic perspectives, this chapter aims to hone in on just what makes Xenakis so politically 'active' – and, apparently paradoxically, what it is about his practice that serves to undermine and disavow the possibilities his work in itself may herald.

It is worth noting here that Xenakis was himself politically active: in 1941, he 'joins the Greek Resistance, first in a right-wing party, then later in the EAM (communist party): he is in the front line of street demonstrations against the occupants, is imprisoned several times, first by the Italians and later by the Germans. His favourite readings include Plato, Marx and Lenin.' (Les Amis de Iannis Xenakis 2014, N. pag.). Therefore, when reading this essay, consider Xenakis not as a name on the shelf of some academic specialist, some composer networking in a dusty echo-chamber, but as at once a mirror and a window sitting alongside the desires espoused by acts of considered vandalism, subversive sexuality, and graffiti such as

> *"Commute, work, commute sleep..." "In a society that has abolished every kind of adventure the only adventure that remains is to abolish the society"; "art is dead, don't consume its corpse."* (Knabb 2006, N. pag.)

May '68 and the Situationist International

In the May of 1968, wildcat protests and strikes, the culmination of the widespread student movement of the time, began to take hold in France, exuding a revolutionary spirit that would end up spreading into all forms of work and social life. These apparently revolutionary acts could perhaps be considered concomitant with the social upheavals of the 1960s and possessed an anti-authoritarian streak, proclaiming that a revolution should be one based on the realisation of the subversive nature of love, and the critique of everyday life and all the phenomena therein that act, consciously or otherwise, in favour of the totality. Eventually, over a million people were marching through the streets of Paris.

Given that a critique of everyday life was a significant part of the foundations of these acts, and is something of a springboard into the perspectives taken on phenomena such as 'art' and what it means in a society like the one in which we live by those who were involved, it is useful to examine just what constitutes the 'everyday life' the students and others found so abhorrent. One of the fundamental tenets of any critique of class society is the critique of the 'administered world', the producer-consumer relationship (that extends to art), and the cessation of chance, in the sense of happenings that are not pre-planned or drawn out of consumption. Such things are demonstrably interrelated with the 'administered world' (as described throughout Theodor W. Adorno and Max Horkheimer's work *Dialectic of Enlightenment*), involving so-called 'risk-assessments' that render spontaneity and chance fundamentally impossible in their truest sense. Due to the hierarchical nature of the division of labour, and the need for such desires to be assuaged, therefore, it fell to the art world, in its moment of autonomy that marked the start of the modernist and avant-garde movements,[1] to act as the 'sphere' in which these things could be allowed to take place. In so doing, the category of 'art' itself became reified – that is, petrified, – into something that could easily be integrated into the bourgeois routine. Art was put to use in order to provide for chance, playfulness, and experimentation abstracted from the praxis of daily life; thus, apparently 'revolutionary' desires were able to be assuaged from within the confines of the totality. While a point of contention for the apparent revolutionaries, they would not hold that art should be subsumed by praxis in that it denotes *action*; rather, the 'praxis' of daily life should, according to the revolutionaries, give itself over to the useful uselessness of artistic behaviour, and what such anti-utilitarianism stands to represent in the possibilities of daily life: '[t]he point is not to put poetry at the service of revolution, but to put revolution at the service of poetry' (Situationist International 2006a). 'Art' as behaviour removed from the praxis of from daily life becomes a restricted, specialist sphere, a limited activity, whose possibilities and experimentation cannot truly take place in a way in which their social consequences could bring themselves to bear (Situationist International 2006b). 'Playfulness' et al. becomes the purview of a privileged group of individuals, often academically trained, or, if not, beholden to poverty through their refusal to give in to the ignominy of earning money.

The capitalist totality, however, is itself hostile to the artistic possibility. Art, therefore, can be sold as a special form of commodity, one in which the 'truly human' may be sensed, making its fetishisation all the more potent, and all the more damaging. There are producers of art, and there are consumers; the latter category constituting the clear majority of those both inside *and* outside the so-called 'art world', made up of both artists and critics. Even then, however, the 'consumers' of art in such a hierarchical society themselves constitute a certain 'niche', a select group who are adept to receive art's 'message in a bottle' (Zuidervaart 1990, 65). How did the Situationist International, and the events of May '68, attempt to challenge this structure of inequality and alienation?

---

[1] This chapter distinguishes between two types of 'avant garde', one a genuine act of artistic progression and spelled using lower case letters, the other an Avant-Garde style and spelled with capitals. For further reading on the topic and this definition, this approach is adopted in Alannah Marie Halay's thesis *Recognising Absurdity: Comparing an Avant-Garde Style with being avant-garde*. See: Halay, A.M. (2016). *Recognising Absurdity through Compositional Practice: Comparing an Avant-Garde Style with being avant-garde*. University of Leeds: PhD.

While their role in instigating the events of May '68 is disputed, the Situationist International rose to prominence in France around that time, having grown in popularity and number since the 1950s out of earlier groups such as the Lettrist International. They espoused libertarian socialist thoughts of an anti-authoritarian, Marxist veneer, finding a home in the 'council communist' tradition that proposed the creation of democratic workers' councils, rather than some form of central government authority or state. Their recognisable bravado and arrogance were directed against both bourgeois moralising and, most importantly of all, what they described as the 'spectacle'. The spectacle constitutes many things, though most presciently it is the advancement of the commodity structure described by Georg Lukács as constituting capitalist society and the human relationships therein. In his seminal work, *History and Class Consciousness*, Lukács (1974, 83-87) ascribes the phenomenon of 'reification' to the dominance of the commodity structure as constitutive of the capitalist totality. The spectacle moves beyond the commodity form such that those relationships are now constituted by images – not necessarily *literal* images, but 'images' meaning 'representations' divorced from experience, and alien to the consumer.[2] The 'image' in this sense acts in a variety of diverse ways. Dependent on the social reality of the commodity structure, the spectacle is made up of a minority of producers, with access to the relevant means of production, and a majority of consumers, whose role it is to stare blankly at the spectacle and to consume its goods, sacrificing their spontaneity and creativity in the process, their imagination curtailed not only by the spectacle itself, but principally by the bourgeois routine from which it springs, and that it constantly rejuvenates. The spectacle is an advancement of the commodity structure in that it accords with the move to the hyperreal, to simulacra, etc. What could once be defined as the apparent relationships between objects masking relationships between human beings, as per Marx's initial summation of the commodity form, have become dominated by ephemeral but ever-present images that extend the fetish component of the commodity structure to an all-consuming totality of alienation where the apparently abstract nature of relationships becomes monetised and reified. The spectacle necessitates a lack of participation, suggested by its 'virtual' existence, its presence-through-absence, and excludes the majority from access to a platform of 'expression' as they become increasingly saturated by the images

---

[2] The capitalist iteration of alienation is dependent upon a whole range of exclusionary, hierarchical practices that result in class distinctions and exploitation. The alienation that results can be described as the alienation from one*self*. Capitalism results in an inability to confront and to love the alien, rendering the dream of the peaceful coexistence of heterogeneous particulars a 'utopian' one.

that constitute the relations of consumption and exchange; essentially the privatisation of all. This is not to suggest that art should be dedicated to so-called 'self-expression'. On the contrary, art as a reified category has become the locus of expression because, within the realm of everyday life, there is no other platform.

The fact that a limited number of people can formally be considered 'artists', and that such practice requires specialised knowledge, ingratiates art into the spectacle and the hierarchical division of labour that keeps late capitalism at work. As previously described, art's function under capitalism as abstracted creativity is to satiate the desires while maintaining the very social relations that create such a specialist sphere in the first place, sustaining a system that ensures all satisfaction remains illusory. It matters not whether the intention of an artist, or a group, is anathema to the social conditions that so restrict them; the totality permits none to stand outside of it, to act as a subject. The fight against the spectacle was one of the integral aspects of the events of May '68; the theoretically literate protesters encouraged the participation of all in the drive towards exploration for the sake of exploration, 'play' as part of everyday life, the valorisation of imagination for its own ends rather than profit and consumption, and the ability for all to be able to explore and play in such ways. It is easy to see the resemblances between the so-called councilist tradition, encouraging worker autonomy, and the fight for participation through emancipated aesthetic forms intent on securing desire for its own sake. In this way, the methods of the Situationist International, and the goals of May '68, constitute an outright rejection of bourgeois art, and the fetishized figure of the artist in that culture.

Chance and the encounter in art as a mass activity open to all were integral, and the methods of Xenakis himself were seen as being wholly compatible with this ethos. Indeed, 'Xenakis, not Gounod' was an example of the graffiti found on the walls of the *Conservatoire National Superieur de Musique de Paris*. The young people taking part in these protests rejected the so-called 'concert ritual', preferring to subject themselves to 'perceptual and aesthetic experimentation.' (M.A. Harley 2005, 64). *Polytope de Cluny*, of course, dates from 1972, but this reveals an ethos at the heart of Xenakis's approach that transcends the apparent limitations of one singular event. What it is therefore integral to explore is just how Xenakis's approach possessed compatibility with the measures that would attempt to emancipate it, and what it is integral to the position of his works, their locus within the category of 'art', that prevents them from reaching their fullest potential.

Chance in music, generally and in that of Xenakis

In a 1957 lecture, *Experimental Music,* John Cage (1973, 12) described music as 'a purposeless play' that can be viewed as 'an affirmation of life – not an attempt to bring order out of chaos nor to suggest improvements in creation, but simply a way of waking up to the very life we're living'. Critical theory abounds that suggests current social structures are themselves imposing a limit on one's ability to 'live', if to live means to play, to experiment, to express, to exercise one's imagination. Cage's assertion could perhaps be related to Adorno's conception of art's 'negative face', turned away from society, aware of its own negativity, wherein lie the possibilities of life.[3] However, for Xenakis, the adoption of chance in music was 'an abuse of language and [...] an abrogation of a composer's function' (Bois and Xenakis 1980, 12). He rejected the notion that the removal of constraints frees the player from habituated responses, believing that the player was still likely to fall back onto convention due to pressure, amongst other things. Chance could not be left entirely to the whims of the composer (Khai-Wei Choong 1996, 32).

Nevertheless, Xenakis *did* adopt chance in his practice, developing what is called 'Stochastic music', that is, an indeterminate approach at the compositional level, allowing for chance to manifest, but only within the terms of a strict mathematical approach, the tools of which are termed 'stochastic distributions' (Tipei 2017). Therefore, Xenakis's approach differed from what might be termed 'Cagean chance', an apparently freer manifestation of chance in composition, through applying a *ratio* to it in an effort to make chance serve the music. Xenakis was not under the illusion that art and specifically music, in its autonomous form, could adopt a form of chance, free of what might be termed aesthetic coherence that would not eventually become stylised and reified. His mathematical approach is itself saturated with epistemic limitations, bowing to the scientific and mathematical developments of the day, and the technology available to the composer's free imagination (Zografos 2017).

Xenakis saw the manifestations of chance and chaos in music as resemblances of chance and chaos in the world at large, as well as refuting the

---

[3] The use of Adorno in this text may seem a contentious inclusion. After all, it is well documented that Adorno was critical of the 'actionism' of the student movement of the 1960s, a critique that came to a head when they occupied his own lecture, resulting in him calling the police on the protestors. His inclusion is excused not only for the fact that distinct resemblances between his aesthetic theory and the views of those discussed here are in evidence, but also for the fact that his work has provided an invaluable window onto an alienated world. Indeed, when the apparently destructive nature of the 1960s movements came to a head, Adorno and the Frankfurt School were reprimanded for inciting them to action, for being their theoretical springboard, even if Adorno did reject the way that his theory was put into practice (Richter & Adorno 2002). When discussing the art and politics of the twentieth century, his philosophy can hardly be ignored.

idea that chance is merely the opposite of reason (Xenakis 1971, 4). His embrace of them within the compositional tools he himself developed was an attempt to harness them in order to explore their role in compositional practice, applying mathematical theories and principles to his music (Zografos 2017). One could, therefore, say that forced chance, that is, chance *sans* a necessary naïveté, is impossible; to suppose that chance could manifest in music without a concerted effort and approach such as Xenakis's stochastic distributions is an illusion.[4] To enforce chance would be to impose a ready-made yet invisible restriction on apparent chance. Xenakis permitted no illusions on this count: chance and chaos would be consciously harnessed in his music without pretence and allowed to function on a mathematical level. This approach *attempts* to avoid the stylisation of chance.

To really understand this position, one must understand the role of 'art' in a capitalist society, in a society where the concert form and its concomitant performer-listener relationship is dominant. The resulting 'specialist sphere' produces an environment in which authorship and 'true chance' are impossible, and where chance is at risk of itself being subsumed into a style; forced chance essentially providing the promissory feeling of spontaneity in a new kind of musical commodity, which allows the system that restricts such spontaneity to essentially be the provider of it in a very limited form, taken into the hierarchical division of labour. In this sense, as above, Xenakis's music provides a window onto an alternative world, with a view that can only be understood through a conception of *this* world. Much of Xenakis's output focused on mixing sound, sight, and space in a combination of the disciplines of architecture and music. A well-known example is the Philips Pavilion project (1958), which featured at the 1958 Brussels World Exposition (Harley 1998, 55). The Philips Pavilion combined sound, colour, light and movement. It was dark inside, and it incorporated one thousand six hundred and eighty strobe lights. Large prisms separated the light of four laser beams, which were then reflected in four hundred mirrors, then reflected further off the floor and glass columns of the pavilion (Xenakis 2008, 56-61). The project featured Xenakis's *Concrèt PH* (1958) and Edgar Varèse's *Poème èlectronique* (1958); both were combined with Le Corbusier's visual display (Harley 1998). Interestingly, Xenakis (2008, 56) did not approve of the collaboration aspect of the Philips Pavilion project and thought that all disparate features should have been brought

---

[4] This subject is discussed at length in Adorno's *Aesthetic Theory*. Also see Halay (2016) for information on naïveté in relation to compositional practice and being 'avant garde' in an 'Avant Garde' world.

together by one creator. This notion is reflected in his later projects, namely *Polytope de Cluny* (1972) (an important piece for the topic at hand), which Xenakis worked on after his collaboration with Le Corbusier had ended.

Whether in collaboration or not, the way Xenakis worked with multiple artistic disciplines seems to reach beyond the Wagnerian 'Gesamtkunstwerk', while also resembling it. The Gesamtkunstwerk could be described as allowing artistic forms to reach beyond the interdisciplinary divisions of art itself, rather than resulting in any true emancipation from the category of 'art' in its current form. What separates Wagner and Xenakis illuminates the difference between Xenakis and the traditional bourgeois artist on a more fundamental level, and announces his compatibility with revolutionary aims. Xenakis's interest in combining music with architecture bespeaks not only an interest in the inherent spatiality of music and its artistic possibilities, but contains within it echoes of a *social* spatiality if one were to compare this aspect of Xenakis's approach with the thought of the Situationist International on what they called 'Unitary Urbanism' (Chtcheglov 2006). In this theory, the 'urban environment' is the physical platform where desires currently confined to what is called 'art' may be enacted, wherein such an environment can be transformed by all who live in it, in the support of the free construction of situations. Therefore, exploring so-called 'artistic behaviour' would occur in such a way that its experiments would influence daily life; indeed, where such experiments would constitute an integral part of daily life. The Wagnerian 'total artwork' is, in this rather brief exposition, an example of a 'revolutionary' artwork that revolutionises nothing other than the potential output of the current mode of artistic production, not the locus of that output nor the ownership of the means. The Gesamtkunstwerk acts as an approbate for bourgeois forms, announcing that nothing is impossible, that all may be included and provided for; the Wagnerian approach in this sense can be said quite simply to act even unconsciously in support of reified, ahistorical categories; a pretence of the universal affirmation and fallacious unity that Xenakis's approach could be harnessed to overcome.

Xenakis's interest in space stemmed from the notion that it could create the possibility of being 'there' while at the same time remaining 'here' (Van Maas 2008, 769). With the proliferation of the spectacle, most people are confined to the 'there', not the 'here', that is, excluded from participation and forced merely to contemplate, to view, where the work they are faced with allows them to do so. For a time, Xenakis worked with Le Corbusier, practising architecture, and, in *Music and Architecture*, he explains how architectural practice can free itself from convention by considering the third dimension, which he calls the "volumetric group" (Xenakis 2008, 111). He incorporated proportional connections between his music and corresponding physical spaces via 'Modulor', the fundamental aspect of architecture that applies the 'golden mean' to the human form, and thus turns the proportions of the body into a measurement that can be applied to all building proportions and form (Matossian 2005, 51). According to Le Corbusier (1978, 6), incorporating the human form into creating Modulor dimensions demonstrated a likeness to long-established measurement schemes, especially the Egyptian Cubit. Xenakis was particularly interested in how Modulor rendered the human form a unifying characteristic of all building proportion, and he considered basing musical composition on the proportions that Modulor comprised (Matossian 2005, 51–52).

An example of Xenakis's application of Modulor into music can be found in the proportional connections between his *Metastasis* (1954) and the Philips Pavilion (Le Corbusier 1978, 326). In *Metastasis*, duration was relative to other musical characteristics: a chromatic scale was sectioned into well-proportioned algebraic intervals, the duration of which determined the moment of their emission and were proportional to these intervals. Geometrical sequences were applied to determine the order of these proportioned intervals as well as the durations themselves (Le Corbusier 1978, 327). The durational format was proportioned by the Fibonacci sequence. The Golden Section's additive characteristic was applied to note durations: durations were added to each other to produce further durations (Matossian 2005, 72). Modulor was also applied to the string glissandi and the number of bars comprising the string glissandi that ended the piece (Xenakis 2008, 46). Xenakis (1971, 10) also used his compositional thinking behind *Metastasis* to design the Philips Pavilion. He wrote that:

> *"If glissandi are long and sufficiently interlaced, we obtain sonic spaces of continuous evolution. It is possible to produce ruled surfaces by drawing the glissandi as straight lines. I performed this experiment with Metastasis [.]"*

The Philips Pavilion demonstrates Xenakis's compositional and architectural prowess, and how these two practices united in his work. The Philips Pavilion became a multi-sensory artwork where space, sound, and sight were catered for. In Xenakis's words:

> *"[W]hen the architect Le Corbusier, whose collaborator I was, asked me to suggest a design for the architecture of the Philips Pavilion in Brussels, my inspiration was pin-pointed by the experiment with Metastasis."*

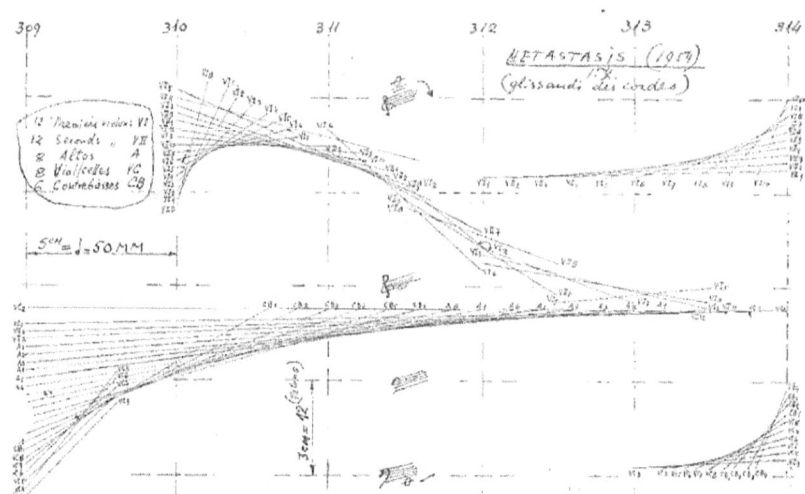

Figure 1.1: Precompositional material for Xenakis's *Metastasis* (1953–54)

The string glissandi in *Metastasis* plotted onto graph paper. This influenced the design of the Philips Pavilion (Xenakis 2008, 99). With kind permission from Pendragon Press.

The way Xenakis described the drawing of string glissandi in *Metastasis* suggests a different way of considering composition: that of architecting the music. Of course, this is not Xenakis's sole attempt to combine music and architecture; as Mariabruna Fabrizi writes, it is his *Polytopes* (1967–78) that 'are the best example of his lifelong ambition in trying to overlap the disciplines'. Fabrizi goes on to explain that the *Polytopes* are tied not to architecture in general, but to a *specific* example or 'archaeological site', searching for "parallel formalisation through the different media", treating each component independently of the others, their synthesis dependent on the spectator-interpreter (Fabrizi 2017, N. pag.).

Premiered in October 1972 in Festival d'Automne, Xenakis's *Polytope de Cluny* played a significant role in the fallout from the May '68 protests. It was composed for The Baths of Cluny in the centre of Paris (Harley 2017). It is useful to refer to it here, then, not only because of its literal significance with regards to the fact the students exposed themselves to it, nor even necessarily due to its espousal of chance. It is the architectural aspects of the piece, its *spatiality*, that are of real interest. In general, the combination of architecture and music offered a fourth dimension to the artwork: according to Le Corbusier (1954, 31), the fourth dimension was the victory of proportion, not just in architecture, but everything. For Xenakis, this fourth dimension in his architectural works allowed perspective and depth of entities, such as the ceiling, walls, and floor, to merge into a unified fold of space, and thus demolished the audience's sense of location (Sterken 2001, 266). The aim of creating another dimension in architecture was able to manifest more strongly with the inclusion of music: according to Le Corbusier (1954, 31), architecture was a realisation of the sounds of 'plastic matter' that created mathematical harmony. Given that Xenakis regarded architecture as 'frozen music', according to Bright (1984, 82), architecture was like music because it, too, comprised entities, which formed a series in time and space (Le Corbusier 1954, 73).

The concept of Modulor dimensions takes on an additional meaning when one factors in thought on the 'urban sphere' and its critique by the Situationist International and others. For instance, for Raoul Vaneigem, 'urbanism', probably best equated to town planning, is an ideology, 'falsely satisfying a falsified need'. He equates it to Guy Debord's notion of the 'spectacle', a life governed by images and representation, as opposed to 'real' experiences, alienating the spectator – or, in this case, the so-called inhabitant' (Kotányi and Vaneigem 2006, N. pag.):

> "Urbanism doesn't exist; it is only an 'ideology' in Marx's sense of the word. Architecture does really exist, like Coca-Cola: though coated with ideology, it is a real production, falsely satisfying a falsified need. Urbanism is comparable to the advertising about Coca-Cola — pure spectacular ideology."

This requires us to think through what the urban means, what *architecture* is, in the current historical moment. Urban spaces are defined by town planners, what the Situationist International calls 'urbanists'; they are developed to sustain the capitalist economy, and their architecture falls in line with profit rather than what might be termed 'human desire'. They are alien, even if they are to be considered artistic. Modulor dimensions work from the proportions of the human body to inform dimensions in architecture. It could be argued that what exists in Xenakis's musical output that corresponds to architecture, for the revolutionary spirit at any rate, is what might be termed 'Modulor desire', the idea that architecture should correspond not only to the physical proportions of the human body, but also their *desires*. Since the urban space is nothing more than a spectacle, such desires cannot be enacted without planning permission and a lot of money. In uniting music with architecture, Xenakis, in an inevitably limited but thoroughly radical way, sought to unite art with the urban, with its social effects. It is Xenakis's *method* that renders it compatible. 'Modulor desire' connects the work of Xenakis with the desires and ideas of 1968: participation, presence, emancipation. Xenakis's uniting of music and architecture paved the way for a unitary urbanism, a world in which architecture was to be designed not for boredom or for profit, but for the satisfaction of creativity, play, and experimentation, aligned with the unique spirit of harnessed chance inherent in his work.

Xenakis and being 'avant garde'

In 'The Culture Industry: Enlightenment as Mass Deception', Adorno and Horkheimer explain how the culture industry, apparently able to cater for every need, has its counterpart in 'avant-garde art', which is likewise able to determine 'its own language'. In this formulation, the avant garde constantly calls for the new and, in so doing, perhaps inadvertently confirms the validity of bourgeois forms in that they are able to be renewed. Nothing can escape the totality constituted by the culture industry and the avant garde. Even so-called mutations of established style are permitted, such that no opposition may be tolerated:

> "Whenever Orson Welles offends against the tricks of the trade, he is forgiven because his departures from the norm are regarded as calculated mutations which serve all the more strongly to confirm the validity of the system." (Adorno and Horkheimer 2016, 128–129)

The way the culture industry is here paired off with the avant garde is striking and telling. As previously stated, art, despite its apparent autonomy from the praxis of daily life, has a position within capitalist society and enacts a form of reification, providing an output for so-called 'radical' tendencies. If the avant garde, and later the Avant Garde (the capitals are used to denote its establishment as a reified style), are seen as being an inescapable part of the capitalist system, at one with the culture industry, then it can be surmised that it is its *negative face*. It still operates on the same producer-consumer basis, and anything new or radical is subsumed. It is not so much that we wish to dismiss the avant garde outright, rather, we intend to reveal the ways in which it is ultimately debased before it even begins. In this way, the avant garde as we know it is a kind of closed sphere, the style known as 'Avant Garde': a select group of specialists enacting the apparent radical will of the majority, reified into predetermined forms. Today, these forms are manifold, given the immediate availability of all past forms. The unifying totality constituted by the Avant Garde, as by the culture industry, ensures that this closed sphere acts as a kind of echo chamber; the restricting of artistic 'progress' to a minimal number of people, inescapably engaged in a competitive form of production, drives forward the stylisation of everything. Halay (2016, 6-7) discusses this at length in her thesis, *Recognising Absurdity: Comparing an Avant-Garde Style with being avant-garde*, which states that:

> "[T]he autonomy of the avant gardes permitted their aging and eventually subsumed them. The historical avant gardes became the Avant Gardes replete with styles, tendencies, specialists, and cut off from their political goals. [...] 'Avant-Garde style' [...] denotes the rationalisation of something previously 'free' (or 'unrestricted', rather). It is the generation of a rule-based system (at the price of its 'aesthetic coherence' as Adorno claimed of 'new music' in 1954). To put it another way, this is the loss of a subversive goal and is 'naïveté of a second order: the uncertainty over what purpose it serves."

'Chance', therefore, in a so-called 'avant-garde' context, would denote this kind of stylisation, patterning, a collection of certain criteria (even if the criteria amounted to the abandonment of criteria): precisely the kind of forced chance that Xenakis balked at. In 'The Avant-Garde of Presence', by the Situationist International (2006b), it is written that:

> "Free play confined within the terrain of artistic dissolution is only the cooption of free play. In spring 1962 the press began reporting on the "happenings" produced by [...] some of the avant-garde artists of New York."

They described such 'happenings' as 'vaguely Dadaist' and an 'improvisation of gestures' carried out within as set of physical boundaries or 'confined space' as they described it. They explain that:

> "This form of social encounter can be considered as an instance of the old artistic spectacle pushed to the extreme, [...] as an attempt to construct a situation in isolation, on a foundation of poverty [.]"

Likewise, in a similar vein, Xenakis rejected:

> "[T]he avant-garde trend of serialism and [built] his own aesthetic principles founded in the world of abstract mathematics, which, amongst other things, applied a unique philosophy of 'chance' to music." (Zografos 2017, N. pag.)

Well-known amongst Xenakis scholars, this became what he called 'stochastic music.' The first two works he composed from these principles were, of course, *Metastasis and Pithoprakta* (1955–56).

Xenakis rejected the trend of serialism, building his principles out of 'the world of abstract mathematics', allowing him to investigate chance in a way absolved of potential ideologisation, committing it to the apparently immutable law of number (Zografos 2017, N. pag.). It is little wonder, therefore, that, with

Xenakis's recognition of the limited nature of avant-garde art in its current situation as determined by the very restrictions it purports to stand against, the students who participated in May '68 found an affinity with his output. This is not to say that Xenakis's work encouraged the participation of all present; rather, there was the germ of something in his method and in the recognition of the very limitations that stunted his own artistry. His music is aware of its own negativity.

From chance to Modulor desire, it is clear that Xenakis's methods are not *in themselves* anathema to the revolutionary intentions and desires of those active in 1968, nor at any other time. Indeed, they could quite conceivably be honed with perfection to the construction of any situation. What Xenakis is not immune to, nor is any other artist, is the previously-described echo chamber that today constitutes the sphere of art. This is an extremely difficult cycle to break out of: any 'successful' method may birth a tendency, any tendency may birth a style, and style results in ageing. Particularly in the age of mechanical reproduction and informatisation, nothing is ephemeral. Works age almost as soon as they are exposed. Even if Xenakis's works were completely anathema to what constituted the so-called 'avant garde' at his time, it was only a matter of time before it became recuperated. Revolutionary desires themselves become compatible with the bourgeois routine, as have the historical avant-garde movements. Xenakis has 'aged': his works are now the province of the Avant Garde, just as those of, say, Schoenberg. This is an important fact to recognise, for it carries with it a bearing on the future practice of musicians and artists of all kinds who wish to be somehow 'radical'. Newness carries prestige, invites esteem, fame, prizes, record labels, Darmstadt, etc. It has become a category, such that it enacts with reified perfection what the Avant Garde, as the flipside of the culture industry, was always ready to do. Newness as a style subsumes all so that newness is no longer possible; as an end in itself, it invokes a betrayal of artistic 'truth'. The point at which the aesthetic approach of Adorno et al. contrasts with the aims of the Situationist International and the participants of May '68 rests in their thoughts on art's stunted ability. While the two are surprisingly similar – Adorno laments the loss of music from the streets in a way that the Situationist International would later echo in their yearning for a new urbanism – the aesthetics of the Situationist International (2006c) call for the *abandonment* of bourgeois art forms, the necessity of *moving beyond* them. Adorno's approach, on the other hand, recognises within 'autonomous art' the presence of a certain political import: the locus of the work's negativity and the challenge to bourgeois forms of consciousness. If we are to suggest Xenakis's approach contains the germ of something revolutionary, while also stating it cannot simply be reduced to 'parody', then there must be something art can achieve, even in its thoroughly debilitated position. Both the Situationist

International and Adorno recognise the impossibility of developing art for the future with the ideological and epistemic limitations of the present; such a move would be doomed to ideological failure, and its aims could never be guaranteed as they can only be tested. The point is to invoke a change in *consciousness*.

It is inevitable that Xenakis may be commodified; even the most subversive artistic approach, in the present, risks faux reconciliation. In her thesis, Halay invokes a new way of imagining originality: the original use of old 'styles', methods, and forms. This is not a directive for the future, rather, it is a call to dispense with the prejudice that arises when one simply 'sounds the same' as anyone else. This prejudice bespeaks the fact that we have forgotten the historical origins of the category of 'art' as it is known today. It is forgetfulness that serves to uphold the reification that condemns art to death.

Bibliography

Adorno, Theodor. W. and Horkheimer, M. 2016. *Dialectic of Enlightenment*. London: Verso. Bois, Mario and Xenakis, Iannis. 1980. *The Man and his Music: A Conversation with the Composer and a Description of his Works*. Westport, CT: Greenwood Press Reprint.

Bright, Michael. 1984. *Cities Built to Music*. Columbus: The Ohio State University Press.

Bürger, Peter. 2002. *Theory of the Avant-Garde*. Minneapolis: University of Minnesota Press.

Cage, John. 1973. *Silence: Lectures and Writings*. Middletown, CT: Wesleyan University Press Paperback.

Choong, Khai-Wei, Xenakis, Iannis and Carter, Elliott. 1996. *A Detailed Examination and Comparative Study of Their Early Output and Creativity*. Brisbane: Griffith University.

Chtcheglov, Ivan. 2017. Formulary for a New Urbanism. http://www.bopsecrets.org/SI/Chtcheglov.htm. (Accessed 20 October 2017).

Fabrizi, Mariabruna. 2017. "Yannis Xenakis' Polytopes: Cosmogonies in Sound and Architecture." http://socks-studio.com/2014/01/08/yannis-xenakis-polytopes-cosmogonies-in-sound-and-architecture. (Accessed 20 October 2017).

Halay, Alannah. Marie. 2016. *Recognising Absurdity through Compositional Practice: Comparing an Avant-Garde Style with being avant-garde*. University of Leeds: PhD.

Harley, James. 2005. *Xenakis: His Life in Music*. New York: Routledge.

Harley, James. 2017. "Xenakis: Polytope de Cluny, for 8-channel tape." http://www.allmusic.com/composition/polytope-de-cluny-for-8-channel-tape-mc0002457509. (Accessed 11 September 2017).

Harley, Maria. Anna. 1998. "Music of Sound and Light: Xenakis's Polytopes." *Leonardo*, 31 (1): 55-65.

Kotányi, Arrila and Vaneigem, Raoul. 2006. "Basic Program of the Bureau of Unitary Urbanism." http://www.bopsecrets.org/SI/6.unitaryurb.htm. (Accessed 20 October 2017).

Le Corbusier. 1954. *The Modulor: A Harmonious Measure to the Human Scale Universally Applicable to Architecture and Mechanics.* Cambridge, MA: Harvard University Press.

Le Corbusier. 1978. *Modulor 2: (Let the User Speak Next) Continuation of 'The Modulor'.* Cambridge, MA: Harvard University Press.

Les Amis de Iannis Xenakis. 2014. "Chronology: 1922-1954." http://www.iannis-xenakis.org/xen/bio/chrono_22-54.html. (Accessed 20 October 2018).

Lukács, Georg. 1974. *History and Class Consciousness: Studies in Marxist Dialectics.* London: Melvin Press.

Matossian, Nouritza. 2005. *Xenakis.* Cyprus: Moufflon Publications.

"May 1968 Graffiti." 2006, edited by Ken Knabb. http://www.bopsecrets.org/CF/graffiti.htm. (Accessed 20 October 2017).

Richter, Gerhard and Adorno, Theodor. W. 2002. "Who's Afraid of the Ivory Tower? A Conversation with Theodor W. Adorno." *Monatshefte,* 94 (1): 10–23.

Situationist International. 2006a. "All the King's Men." http://www.bopsecrets.org/SI/8.kingsmen.htm. (Accessed 20 October 2017).

Situationist International. 2006b. "The Avant Garde of Presence." http://www.bopsecrets.org/SI/8.avantgarde.htm. (Accessed 20 October 2017).

Situationist International. 2006c. "A User's Guide to Détournement." http://www.bopsecrets.org/SI/detourn.htm. (Accessed 20 October 2017).

Sterken, Sven. 2001. "Towards a Space-Time Art: Iannis Xenakis's Polytopes." *Perspectives of New Music,* 39 (2): 262-273.

Tipei, Sever. 2017. "Chance Music." http://ems.music.illinois.edu/courses/tipei/M202/Notes/cage1.html. (Accessed 20 October 2017).

Van Maas, Sander. 2008. "Intimate Exteriorities: Inventing Religion Through Music." In *Religion: Beyond a Concept,* edited by Hent de Vries. New York: Fordham University Press.

Xenakis, Iannis. 1971. *Formalized Music: Thought and Mathematics in Composition.* Bloomington: Indiana University Press.

Xenakis, Iannis. (2008). *Music and Architecture.* Translated, compiled and presented by Sharon Kanach. New York: Pendragon Press.

Zografos, Markos. (2017). *Iannis Xenakis: the aesthetics of his early works.* http://www.furious.com/perfect/xenakis.html. (Accessed 20 October 2017).

Zuidervaart, Lambert. (1990). "The Social Significance of Autonomous Art: Adorno and Bürger." *The Journal of Aesthetics and Art Criticism,* 48 (1): 61-77.

Part II - Compositional practice

Chapter 2

The Berlin sketches and Xenakis's middle-period style

Dimitris Exarchos

Introduction

Beyond some private tuition that he received in his early age, Iannis Xenakis was largely an autodidact composer. This is perhaps part of the reason why his musical thinking relied heavily on ideas outside music. Architectural and mathematical ideas seem to have informed his early work more so than his later music. This chapter explores such ideas and the ways they have shaped the style of Xenakis's music through the years, especially the 1960s and 1970s. His original compositional approach in his 'opus 1', *Metastaseis* (1953-54), comprised a discovery – that of mass sonorities – linked to the architectural texture of ruled surfaces. The mathematics that enabled further control of such mass phenomena came later, with *Pithoprakta* (1955-56) and *Achorripsis* (1956-57). These works exemplified what came to be called *stochastic music*. To the extent that stochastics refer to a particular compositional approach and invite a particular way of listening, we can say that the term *stochastic* refers to Xenakis's early-period style.

The question of style is not only technical but relies on several factors. However, the technical aspect can help identify some underlying ideas that may have influenced several works for long periods of time. The novelty of new methodologies may have generated material that was later used in other works. Gibson (2011) has closely studied the practice of self-borrowing (*montage*) in Xenakis. The first work to heavily borrow material from preceding ones is *Duel* (1959), followed by *Hiketides* (1964) and more works with increasing frequency after that. Self-borrowing creates a strong sense of stylistic continuity, and thus locating the landmarks and breakthroughs in Xenakis's works helps periodisation. This chapter argues that each new compositional landmark (a discovery in compositional technique) effectuated a stylistic evolution; however, I also attempt to locate a deeper compositional thinking that potentially unifies stylistic differences, thus providing higher-level connections between periods, ranging from Xenakis's early to his late years. More specifically, I argue that at the origins of the middle period, there lies a major discovery of a theory that encompasses Xenakis's thinking until his late music, and that it can retrospectively refer to his early-period work; namely, the discovery of outside-time musical structures. I will do so by analysing the sketches of the period of Xenakis's residency in Berlin in 1963-64. This analysis testifies to the genesis of the theory of outside-time structures and the close link this has to Xenakis's compositional methods of sets, sieves, and groups. Combined with analysis of the later music, this theory is shown to apply to broader stylistic categories than technical compositional methods.

Period	Work	Method	Matossian (1981)	Solomos (1996)	Harley (2004)
	pre *Metastaseis*			Bartókian	
Early	*Metastasis* (1953-54)	Mass sonorities	Stochastic	Epic	Architecture / Algorithm
	Pithoprakta (1955-56)	Stochastics			
	Achorripsis (1956-57)	Stochastics			
	Duel (1959)	Game Theory			
Middle: Formali-sation	*Herma* (1961)	Sets, Symbolic Logic	Formali-sation	Utopian	
	Akrata (1964-65)	Groups, Sieves			Voice/ Stage/ Time
	Nomos alpha (1965-66)	Groups, Sieves			
	Persephassa (1969)	Rhythmic sieves			
Middle: Bricolage	*Synaphaï* (1969)	(Arborescences)	Branching out		Arborescences/ Random walks/ Cosmic conceptions
	Mikka (1971)	Brownian Motion			
	Evryali (1973)	Arborescences			
Late	*Jonchaies* (1977)	Halo Sonorities, New Sieves		Interiorisation	Sieves/ Ensembles
	Aïs (1980)	Random Sieves			
	Horos (1986)	Cellular Automata			Melody/ Harmony/ Form
	Ergma (1994)	?			Abstraction/ Intensity

Table 2.1: Periodisation of Xenakis's work

Periodisation

Solomos (2008), Matossian (2005), and Harley (2004) have all provided periodisations that tend to coincide. What I am proposing here is complementary to these. Specifically, I propose that looking at compositional landmarks we could designate the periods of Xenakis's work as shown on the left-hand side of Table 2.1.

Early period

The early period is clearly marked by *Metastaseis*, although Xenakis had composed works before that too (see Solomos 2002). The idea of mass sonorities, as mentioned, relates to architecture and was also applied in Xenakis's Philips Pavillion in Burssels' expo of 1958. The mass structures were drawn 'architecturally', but the formal application of probabilities came with *Pithoprakta*. Xenakis here borrows from mathematician Jacques Bernouli the term *stochastic*, to refer to a kind of process whereby the listening gathers the tendency towards a target, but not the local detail (from the Greek 'stochos', which means 'target'). The overall form of *Pithoprakta* progresses from randomly-distributed noisy and percussive sounds, to orderly-distributed clear, held harmonics. On a smaller scale, the idea of 'throwing sound' via 'stochastic composition, that of the minimum of constraints and rules' (Xenakis 1992, 134), came with *Achorripsis*, which is not based on mass sonorities, but achieves formal balance via appropriate distribution of local events according to procedures of a given average; thus, the 'target' is now the formal articulation of the work on its various levels. The stochastic experience will reach its highest formalisation with the *ST*-family of five works (1956-62), where a 'black-box' stochastic process is set up for each work, and the composer only enters the initial data, such as instrumentation, sound types, etc.

Middle period

The middle period is here further sub-divided into two sub-periods, according to Xenakis's working methods.

Formalisation. The first half of the middle period (roughly, the 1960s) is characterised by high formalisation, which gave rise to new theories and musical structures; the origins of this period is the focus of the following sections of this article. The main methods here are those of Sets (what Xenakis called 'Symbolic Logic'), Sieves, and Groups. The latter, as I will show, although comprise a distinct theory in Xenakis's work, also relate to sieves; thus, groups were used to create either outside-time structures, such as sieves, or inside-time structures, such as sound-to-sound procedures.

Bricolage. The second half of the middle period is clearly less formalised. I am following here Solomos's (2005) suggestion of the term *bricolage*, which indicates the idea and practice of handiwork as theorised by Claude Levi Strauss. This second part of the middle period introduced new compositional tools, such as graphics, whereby the composer either freely composed graphic schemata, or created these via probabilistic computational processes, before transferring and transcribing them into musical ideas and notation. The first signs of such method are found in *Synaphaï*. In its early stages these graphs stemmed out of Xenakis's experiments on sound synthesis via directly composing the wave form (see Xenakis 1992, 246); however, the realisation of these ideas had had to wait as the computational power available at the time was not enough. Such is the case of *Mikka* (see Solomos 2001b), which is inspired by the random movement of the molecules in gases, formalized by simple probabilistic tools ('Brownian motion' or 'Random walk'). In *Evryali* this approach is fleshed-out in the form of arborescences, that is, multiple Brownian-motion lines that branch out of one another, giving rise to Xenakis's take on polyphony. These structures may have had a computational background, but the application on instrumental music had the sense of bricolage, rather than a formalised process. Thus, formalisation and bricolage stand opposed to one another, although as I will show later, Xenakis considered all of his work (with the exception of the *ST* family) to be of the latter kind.

Late period

All three periods overlap and although there are distinct characteristics to each, there is not always a clear demarcation line. One example is the use of glissandi, which effectively disappeared from Xenakis's music in the 1980s, although the string quartet of 1983 *Tetras* makes extensive use of these. This period, which Solomos (2008) describes as one of 'interiorisation' can be roughly designated by a renewed treatment of older methods as well as the introduction of new aesthetics and compositional methods (often combined with older ones). The first work to introduce such new ideas is *Jonchaies*, which relies on a new conception of sieves and the introduction of a heterophony that Xenakis (1977: preface) described as 'artificial reverberation' and Solomos (1996) termed 'halo sonority'. The new pitch scales of the late period belong to a class of sieves, which I have termed the *Xenakis Sieve* (Exarchos, Forthcoming); this sieve is the outcome of a reinvention of sieve theory with the use of probabilities, and as a construct it is based on a *random sieve* which retains a certain set of characteristics in terms of range and distribution of intervals, thus rendering a typical sound-world of pitch and mass sonorities. In the late period, these mass sonorities are not based on glissandi, but on clusters of sounds on the work's sieve(s). These two approaches will be typical of many works to follow. Combined with these (halo sonorities and random sieves) Xenakis made use also of cellular automata: iterative processes of a simple repeated rule that result in complex structures, indexing Xenakis's conception of sound as 'a kind of fluid in time' (Varga 1996, 200). Finally, Xenakis moved to more austere, perhaps esoteric abstractions in his works of the 1990s, such as *Ergma* or *Ittidra* (1996) - what Harley (2004) described using the terms *abstraction* and *intensity* (see Table 1). Although some of these late works have been analysed (e.g., Solomos 2001c), at present they seem to be resistant to specific theories or working methods.

Origins of the middle-period style

As is well known, Xenakis's polemic against serialism relates to his own stochastic approach. 'La crise de la musique sérielle' was published in 1955, between his effective opuses 1 and 2 (*Metastaseis* and *Pithoprakta*). Serialism was exposed as a limiting combinatorial effort by composers who in vain tried to handle the musical surface by purely linear means. Further, if composing with twelve notes was a kind of combinatorics, why not generalise this to include more than just twelve notes? Or, why limit one's options to permutation and not include all possible combinations? Thus, *stochastics* was the radical generalisation of combinatorics. Not only the range of options was extended to include the entire domain of pitch (as opposed to pitch-class), stochastics also included various layers of polyphony so as to control masses of sound. In other words, rather than simply rotating a limited set, stochastics offered the tools to control a large population of elements, where the only limit is that of audibility. Historically, what Xenakis called 'inside-time' operations met their fullest actualisation with the abandoning of the scale by free-atonality and subsequently by serialism. Stochastics effected a 'hypertrophy' of the inside-time category, which 'became overwhelming and arrived at a dead end' (*FM* 208); thus bringing the early period to a close. The term 'inside-time' was formulated at a later stage and was used by Xenakis to refer to the above only retrospectively. This hypertrophy of the inside-time was a deathblow to any music that insisted ignoring the deeper structure of music that is atemporal; and it helped spark Xenakis's middle period, which begins at the moment of his next discovery, that of outside-time structures.

In his writings, this discovery is documented for the first time in the last chapter of *Musiques Formelles*.[1] This chapter ('Musique Symbolique') includes

---

[1] *Musiques Formelles* (Xenakis 1963) is a collection of articles published in 1963 as volumes 253-254 of Revue Musicale, reprinted as chapters I-VI in Xenakis 1992.

an analysis of the sets and their treatment in *Herma* (1960-61). In *Formalized Music*, this chapter (VI) along with chapters VII and VIII, attempts to 'go at the bottom of things' with the aid of logic and mathematics (Xenakis 1992, 208). This new attempt at a higher formalisation that distinguishes between inside and outside of time marks the beginning of the middle period. My focus here is on the genesis of these ideas which first became manifest in *Akrata* and to a greater extent in *Nomos alpha*.

Xenakis's conception of outside-time structure is complex, mainly due to his mode of presentation that took different forms between several of his writings. His best example for the outside-time category is, I believe, what in mathematics is known as 'totally ordered structure', a structure whereby, "given three elements of one set, you are able to put one of them in between the other two" (Zaplitny 1975, 97). In other words, a structure is outside of time when "you can arrange all the elements into a room full of the other elements," according to "some comparative adjective: bigger, larger, smaller," "higher in pitch", or even "later in time" (Zaplitny 1975, 97).

The Berlin residency & sketches

Between October 1963 and September 1964 Xenakis was resident in Berlin, on a grant awarded by the Ford Foundation and the West-Berlin Senate (see Xenakis 1992, 371). The sketches produced during his residency offer insight to his thinking during this period of gestation. The musical aesthetic that this period gave rise to is evident in a variety of ways in the middle and late periods. The music works that immediately followed *Herma* rely heavily on ideas to which the sketches testify; these ideas were expressed in the articles that followed *Musique Formelles*. In these notes, the discovery of outside-time structures takes the form the mathematical property of *commutativity*, according to which the combination of two objects is independent of their order. In musical terms, constructs that make use of this property are scales and sets, however, Xenakis initially made the discovery on the technical level. In his mathematical notes, he struggled for sometime before he could arrive at a double conclusion: that the composer may decompose a structure into its constituent elements, in such a way that the order of these elements does not matter. This double discovery is that of *decomposition* and *commutativity*. His journey into this realisation starts with the sets of *Herma*. The 'symbolic music' of *Herma* unfolds a predetermined logical process of combining three sets, A, B, and C, via the operations of union (+), intersection (*), and complementation (−), as shown in Figure 1 (see Xenakis 1963, 206 & 1992, 170-7).

The Berlin sketches and Xenakis's middle-period style 27

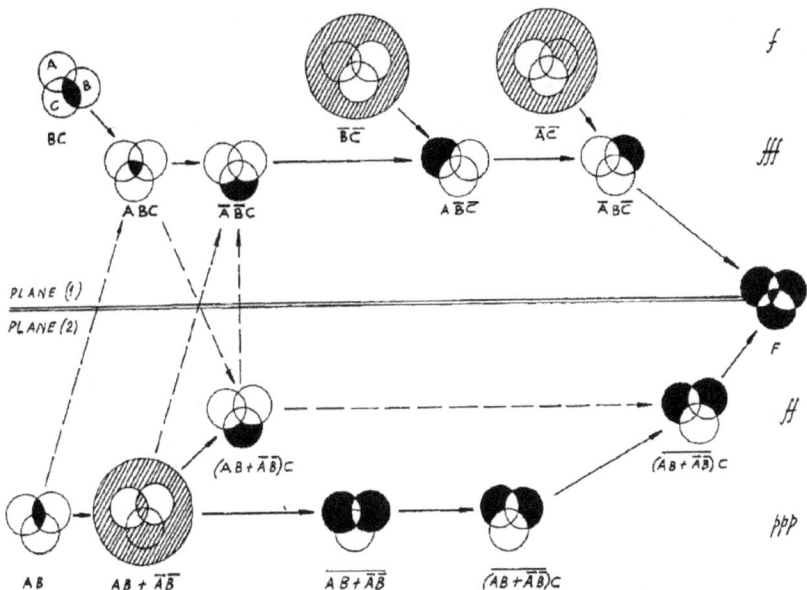

Figure 2.1: Flow Chart of *Herma*
With kind permission from Pendragon Press.

As I have shown in Exarchos, Forthcoming, the work done for *Herma* was developed towards the compositions that followed, so as to include the aforementioned discoveries. In *Akrata*, the first product of the Berlin residency, Xenakis applied these operations to *residue classes*, rather than sets. (He retained the same labels, A, B, and C, when he worked these out in the sketches.) A *residue class* (RC), notated by a pair (M, I), is a series of multiples of a unit, consisting of numbers that give the same residue when divided by M. For example, 4, 7, and 10 all give residue 1 when divided by 3. This relation is symbolised by '≡':

$$1 \equiv 4(mod 3) \equiv 7(mod 3) \equiv 10(mod 3)$$

If middle C is set to 0 and the unit is the semitone, the example above is a diminished 7th configuration starting on C#: (3, 1) = C# E G B♭... Working with RC's allowed Xenakis to either construct scales by combining RC's with the functions mentioned above, or to analyse a given scale by decomposing its overall periodicity into elementary ones; this is the groundwork for Sieve Theory.

In *Herma* sets A, B, and C, are irregular pitch scales spanning the whole piano range. In *Akrata* the same labels stand for moduli (M): $A = 2$, $B = 3$, and $C = 5$. In the pre-compositional stages for both works these are combined in the following ways, producing eight sieves (although not all were used):

$$\alpha = ABC \qquad\qquad \alpha' = \overline{A}BC$$
$$\beta = AB\overline{C} \qquad\qquad \beta' = \overline{A}B\overline{C}$$
$$\gamma = A\overline{B}C \qquad\qquad \gamma' = \overline{AB}C$$
$$\delta = A\overline{BC} \qquad\qquad \delta' = \overline{ABC}$$

where the three classes are combined via intersection and the overline sign stands for complementation (e.g., $\bar{A}$ = all the pitches not in A). As Schaub (2005) has shown, *Akrata* employs scales based on the above RC's, as well as further transformations (e.g., $\delta_0 + A_1$, $\delta 1 + A_0$, $\delta 0 + B_0$, where the subscript stands for *I*).

Sketches consulted

The dossiers in the Xenakis Archive that are relevant to this chapter are the following:

- Œuvres Musicales 19/14 [Sieves]
    - Sieve calculations and graphic transcriptions of passages from works by Ravel and Chopin.
- Œuvres Musicales 19/17 [Sieves - Berlin period]
    - Sieve and group calculations
- Œuvres Musicales 19/18 [Sieves - Berlin period]
    - Sieve and group calculations, including rotations of the cube
- Œuvres Musicales 19/19 [Sieves & Groups - Berlin period]
    - Sieve and group calculations, including rotations of the tetrahedron
- Œuvres Musicales 19/20 [Sieves - Berlin period]
    - Sieve and group calculations, including analysis of Messiaen's modes

The mathematical aspects of these concern mainly three topics: sets, sieves, and groups. Sets, as mentioned were employed in *Herma*, and in *Akrata*

Xenakis introduced sieves, which are predominantly pitch-scales, but can also be, and have been, rhythmic sequences (such as in *Persephassa*). Groups are special collections of objects, which form a closed set of elements that is equipped with a function. As the sketches testify, Xenakis spent a lot of time to study these from Ledermann 1979 (first published in the late 1940s), and used them equally for the conception of sieves (outside of time) and for determining sequences of events (inside time).

Sieves

The most common form of a sieve is that of a pitch scale; less common, but equally possible is a time-point scale. Therefore, any scale is a sieve; however, the latter is a generalisation of the former. In fact, a sieve is a class of scales; that is, it includes all the possible transformations that leave its internal (intervallic) structure unchanged. These transformations are namely that of cyclic transposition (a shift that causes the scale to start on some other point of its intervallic structure) and that of retrograde (where the intervallic structure is inverted). For example, the white-key modes are all cyclic transpositions of one single sieve (see Xenakis 1992, 268). More generally, the term sieve refers to a series of points on a line (a 'well-ordered structure'), regardless of the process that gave rise to it or of its mathematical expression. In the Berlin sketches, the basic constituent elements of sieves are invariably RC's; these may be combined with set-theoretical operations, but their moduli (M) may be provided by groups. Xenakis's definition for a sieve is appropriately general: a sieve is 'every well-ordered set [that] can be represented as points on a line, as long as a reference point is given for the origin and a length u for the unit distance' (Xenakis 1992, 268).

Groups

Groups are special collections of objects that satisfy certain properties, given a law of composition. The main property of groups is that of *closure*: the combination of any two members always results in another member of the same group. Among its other properties (see Ledermann 1979, 1-4), there is an additional one that may or may not be satisfied, that of *commutativity*, according to which, for each element it is true that

$$AB = BA$$

Such groups are called commutative, or abelian[2] and constitute structures outside of time. Commutativity helps distinguish between two kinds of groups:

1. Abelian groups: multiplicative and additive groups

2. Non-abelian groups: such as symmetry groups, or groups of permutations

As shown in Exarchos, Forthcoming, Xenakis's discovery of decomposition and commutativity during his Berlin residency happened when researching the former kind, and in particular additive groups. However, he first seems to have started with the multiplicative kind.

Multiplicative Groups. The residues of M that are prime relative to M form a finite abelian group with respect to multiplication modulo M. Two numbers are relatively prime when their greatest common divisor is 1. For example, if $M = 15$, group $M15$ consists of the numbers smaller than 15 that are prime relative to 15:

$$M15 = 1, 2, 4, 7, 8, 11, 13, 14$$

The law of composition is multiplication followed by reduction modulo 15 (see Table 2. 2).

		I	A	A^2	AB	A^3	B	A^3B	A^2B
	x	1	2	4	7	8	11	13	14
I	1	1	2	4	7	8	11	13	14
A	2	2	4	8	14	1	7	11	13
A^2	4	4	8	1	13	2	14	7	11
AB	7	7	14	13	4	11	2	1	8
A^3	8	8	1	2	11	4	13	14	7
B	11	11	7	14	2	13	1	8	4
A^3B	13	13	11	7	1	14	8	4	2
A^2B	14	14	13	11	8	7	4	2	1

Table 2.2: Matrix for multiplicative group M15, where $A = 2$ and $B = 11$

---

[2] After mathematician Niels Henrik Abel.

The Berlin sketches and Xenakis's middle-period style

In dossier O.M. 19/17, Xenakis studied the properties of groups of different sizes, such as $M12$, $M10$, $M18$, and $M21$. Xenakis's first meaningful attempt to decomposition aimed at the internal structure of the group, the level of 'hidden' symmetries that he referred to (1992, 269-270). This was achieved via decomposing a group into sub-groups. In all finite groups, some power of an element is equal to the unit element.

In $M15$,

$$2^4 = 16$$

and

$$16 \, (mod\, 15) \equiv 1$$

Groups whose elements can all be expressed as powers of a single element are called cyclic. The cyclic sub-group generated by 2 is closed precisely because $2^4 \, (mod\, 15) \equiv 1$:

$$1, 2^1, 2^2, 2^3, 2^4 \equiv 1, 2, 4, 8, 1$$

The subgroup generated by 11 can be combined to produce the whole group:

$$1, 11^1, 11^2 \equiv 1, 11, 1$$

The product of the two subgroups is achieved by multiplying each element in the one sub-group by all other elements in the other sub-group:

$$1, 2, 4, 8, 11, 22, 44, 88$$

and reduced according to modulo 15 we have the original group:

$$M15 = 1, 2, 4, 8, 11, 7, 14, 13$$

However, this kind of decomposition was not successful for practical reasons. The composer needs to be able to substitute the factors for the original modulus (15 in this case, or 12 for the sieve of the traditional modes). When this is applied to multiplicative groups, the intersection of factors produces only one point of the sieve within the period of 15. Thus, Xenakis turned his attention to additive groups.

Additive Groups. Additive groups include not only the relatively-prime, but all integers smaller than M. For additive group $M15$ the two sub-groups that suffice to reproduce the whole group with respect to addition modulo 15, are all the multiples of 3 and all the multiples of 5:[3]

$$3, 6, 9, 12, 0$$

and

$$5, 10, 0$$

That is, the original additive group $M15$ is the result of all possible sums (modulo 15) of the elements of the two sub-groups above. These, of course, are effectively RC's (3, 0) and (5, 0), and according to Group Theory, they comprise the unique decomposition of this group (see Table 2.3).

		I	A^2B^2	A^4B	A	A^3B^2	B	A^2	A^4B^2	AB	A^3	B^2	A^2B	A^4	AB^2	A^3B
	+	0	1	2	3	4	5	6	7	8	9	10	11	12	13	14
I	0	0	1	2	3	4	5	6	7	8	9	10	11	12	13	14
A^2B^2	1	1	2	3	4	5	6	7	8	9	10	11	12	13	14	0
A^4B	2	2	3	4	5	6	7	8	9	10	11	12	13	14	0	1
A	3	3	4	5	6	7	8	9	10	11	12	13	14	0	1	2
A^3B^2	4	4	5	6	7	8	9	10	11	12	13	14	0	1	2	3
B	5	5	6	7	8	9	10	11	12	13	14	0	1	2	3	4
A^2	6	6	7	8	9	10	11	12	13	14	0	1	2	3	4	5
A^4B^2	7	7	8	9	10	11	12	13	14	0	1	2	3	4	5	6
AB	8	8	9	10	11	12	13	14	0	1	2	3	4	5	6	7
A^3	9	9	10	11	12	13	14	0	1	2	3	4	5	6	7	8
B^2	10	10	11	12	13	14	0	1	2	3	4	5	6	7	8	9
A^2B	11	11	12	13	14	0	1	2	3	4	5	6	7	8	9	10
A^4	12	12	13	14	0	1	2	3	4	5	6	7	8	9	10	11
AB^2	13	13	14	0	1	2	3	4	5	6	7	8	9	10	11	12
A^3B	14	14	0	1	2	3	4	5	6	7	8	9	10	11	12	13

Table 2.3: Matrix for additive group $M15$, where $A = 3$ and $B = 5$

---

[3] Note that in $mod15$-space $15 \equiv 0$.

This is the moment of the genesis of Sieve Theory as this was later formulated and presented in articles such as 'Towards a Metamusic' of 1967 (reproduced in Xenakis 1992)[4]. In the sketches, Xenakis worked on graph paper for his tables and sieves represented as points on a straight line. Often he used the back of these graph sheets to jot down ideas and further calculations. On the back page of such a graph paper, where he studied groups as a multiplicative and additive, Xenakis notes that $z = x_i + y_i$, where x and y stand for moduli 3 and 5 (and i refers to the I of an RC). Over all these pencil calculations, Xenakis noted in red ink: 'Eureka' and 'Berlin, 28/6/64, 5pm'.[5] This is then the birth moment of sieves and of outside-time structures (on the technical level), which were conceived as 'any group, which entails an additive operation and whose elements are multiples of unity' (Xenakis 1992, 268; see Exarchos, Forthcoming).

	Outside Time	Inside Time
Early		Stochastics
		Game Theory
Middle: *Formalization*	Symbolic Logic	Symbolic Logic
	Sets	
	Groups	Groups
	Sieves	
Middle: *Bricolage*		Brownian motion
		Arborescences
Late		Cellular Automata
		Granular Synthesis
		Dynamic Stochastic Synthesis

Table 2.4: Periodisation of Xenakis's compositional methods according to the dichotomy Outside/Inside-Time

Continuity

As is well documented, Xenakis used Group Theory also to construct inside-time structures, such as cyclic paths or symmetry groups (non-abelian groups

---

[4] The manuscript of 'Towards a Metamusic' dates from December 1965 and is titled 'Harmoniques (Structures hors-temps)' (see Solomos 2001a)

[5] Dossier O.M. 19/17, p.2; Greek in the original.

of permutations). Both of these are known from his own analyses of *Nomos alpha* and *Nomos gamma*, which are presented from the two aspects of outside- and inside-time (Xenakis 1992, 219-241). Further, the compositional methods that followed corresponded mostly to the inside-time category, but Xenakis always kept developing and combining his methods. A summary of these is shown in Table 2. 4. Each one of these methods is further categorized according to its nature as outside- or inside-time.

Xenakis's work exhibits a great sense of variety, but also of continuity. This chapter argues that, on a deeper level, such continuity can be accounted for by Xenakis's compositional methodology, which distinguishes between two kinds of structure, as the two main dimensions of his compositional work. Xenakis himself frequently made a point by privileging the outside-time aspect of music; however, this was partly a corrective move: his main aim was to emphasise what the history of music seemed to have neglected. Both of these two aspects are significant in different ways, and his working methods relied on both in equally important ways. These two kinds of structure enabled a compositional thinking that spanned decades and provided large-scale connections in Xenakis's oeuvre. It is characteristic that *Formalized Music* (1992) begins and ends with chapters on Stochastics (the hypertrophy of the inside-time). Similarly, his later electroacoustic works mark a return to stochastics. One reason for this may be the advent of technology: while the 'actions with probabilities' of *Pithoprakta* were made by hand, the *ST* works were calculated by way of a 'black box'; and the late electroacoustic works such as *Gendy* and *S.709* were produced via purely algorithmic processes (this time on the microstructure of the sound itself). Xenakis's vision remained so persistent that he never seemed to abandon a theory: he kept employing sieves, groups, cellular automata, etc. Also, over the years he seemed to have internalised or automated some of his original methods; a stochastic passage may have been composed intuitively, or his sieves produced by random algorithmic processes.

Xenakis's radical abstraction and his attempt to 'go at the bottom of things' took the form of high formalisation. However, it is known that his use of mathematics was never strictly formal. Himself referred to his work as 'handiwork'; all of his works (apart from the *ST* family)

> "are mostly handiwork, in the biological sense: adjustments that cannot be controlled in their totality. If God existed He would be a handyman."
> (Xenakis 1987, 23)

His theory of temporality was compositionally as important as his mathematical formalisation. An engineer by training, Xenakis defined himself as a *bricoleur*. Mathematics is the means to achieving an aesthetic goal that would not have been achieved purely intuitively. It seems that over the years experience turned formalisation into style. What is most interesting here is precisely the persistence of a vision that found its way into Xenakis's works via renewed methodologies and a reconception of the temporal categories.

Acknowledgments

The research that led to this paper was conducted partly under my residency at the National Institute for Music Research in Berlin between May and August 2013, a fellowship funded by the Prussian Cultural Heritage Foundation. I am grateful to Mâkhi Xenakis for allowing me to consult the Xenakis archive and the help of Pierre Carré. I am also thankful to Marie-Gabrielle Soret for her assistance while consulting the Bibliothèque Nationale de France, where the archive was previously held.

Bibliography

Exarchos, Dimitris. 2018. "On The Evolution of Xenakis's Compositional Thinking." In *Perspectives on Greek Musical Modernism*, edited by Eva Mantzourani, Costas Tsougras and Petros Vouvaris. London; New York: Routledge. Forthcoming.

Gibson, Benoît. 2011. *The Instrumental Music of Iannis Xenakis: Theory, Practice, Self-Borrowing*. Hillsdale, New York: Pendragon Press.

Harley, James. 2004. *Xenakis: His Life in Music*. New York; London: Routledge.

Ledermann, Walter. 1979. *Introduction to Group Theory*. London: Longman.

Matossian, Nouritza. 2005. *Xenakis*. Lefkosia: Moufflon Publications.

Schaub, Stéphane. 2005. "Akrata, for 16 winds by Iannis Xenakis: Analyses." In *Definitive Proceedings of the International Symposium Iannis Xenakis (Athens, May 2005)*, edited by Makis Solomos, Anastasia Georgaki, and Giorgos Zervos. http://www.iannis-xenakis.org/Articles/Schaub.pdf

Solomos, Makis. 2001a. "Bibliographie commentée des écrits de/sur Iannis Xenakis." In *Présences de / Presences of Iannis Xenakis*, edited by Makis Solomos, 231-265. Paris, Centre de documentation de la musique contemporaine.

Solomos, Makis, 2001b. "The Unity of Xenakis's Instrumental and Electroacoustic Music: The case of 'Brownian Movements'." *Perspectives of New Music* 39 (1): 244-54.

Solomos, Makis. 2001c. "Notes sur les derniéres œuvres de Xenakis." In *Présences de / Presences of Iannis Xenakis*, edited by Makis Solomos, 59-64. Paris, Centre de documentation de la musique contemporaine.

Solomos, Makis. 2002. "Xenakis' Early Works: From 'Bartókian Project' to 'Abstraction'." *Contemporary Music Review* 21(2-3): 21-34.

Solomos, Makis. 2005. "Cellular Automata in Xenakis's music. Theory and Practice." In *Definitive Proceedings of the International Symposium Iannis Xenakis (Athens, May 2005)*, edited by Makis Solomos, Anastasia Georgaki,

Giorgos Zervos http://cicm.mshparisnord.org/ColloqueXenakis/papers/Solomos.pdf

Solomos, Makis. 2008. *Iannis Xenakis: to sympan henos idiotypou demiourgou*. Athens: Alexandreia.

Varga, Bálint András. 1996. *Conversations with Iannis Xenakis*. London: Faber and Faber.

Vriend, Jan. 1981. "Nomos Alpha for Violoncello Solo (Xenakis 1966). Analysis and Comments." *Interface: Journal of New Music Research* 10(1): 15-82.

Xenakis, Iannis. 1963. "Musique Formelles", *Revue Musicale*, 253-254.

Xenakis, Iannis. 1977. *Jonchaies*. Paris: Éditions Salabert.

Xenakis, Iannis. 1987. "Xenakis on Xenakis." *Perspectives of New Music* 25(1): 16-63.

Xenakis, Iannis. 1992. *Formalized Music*. Edited by Sharon Kanach. NY: Pendragon Press.

Zaplitny, Michael. 1975. "Conversation with Iannis Xenakis." *Perspectives of New Music* 14(1): 86-103.

Chapter 3

Stratification of sound masses in Xenakis's *Gmeeoorh* (1974)

Marina Sudo

Introduction

Quality of sound is the consequence of synthesised parameters such as pitch, loudness, timbre or density. These parameters interact with each other, and a small difference in one parameter can effect significant change to the resulting musical sound. It is this essential fact about sound that throughout the twentieth-century accelerated the drastic shift of compositional concern from intervallic/harmonic organisation to integration of elementary properties and functions of sound. In particular, the importance of *sonoristic* perspectives came to be fully appreciated; this is the case even in the music by the 'post-Webernian' serial composers, who pursued the system primarily based upon intervallic logic despite their considerable interest in timbre. Iannis Xenakis is one of the composers who not only appreciated the significance of parameter difference of musical sounds but also established their own styles in deep contemplation of the elementary sonic profile. In order to design the overall sound on a blank canvas, Xenakis often used graphic sketching at the first step of composition, from which his sonic imagination was concretised as a reflection of microstructure. In the chapter of 'Towards a philosophy of music' from *Formalized music* (1992) seven categories of general qualities are suggested as the elements that construct the 'sonic fields' represented in graphic outline of sound masses:

"1. Registers (medium, shrill, etc.)

2. Overall density (large orchestra, small ensemble, etc.)

3. Overall intensity

4. Variation of timbre (arco, sul ponticello, tremolo, etc.)

5. Fluctuations (local variations of 1, 2, 3, 4 above)

6. *General progress of the form (transformation into other elementary forms)*

7. *Degree of order (Total disorder can only make sense if it is calculated according to the kinetic theory of gases. Graphic representation is the most convenient for this study)".*
(Xenakis 1992, 213)

Whilst providing important perspectives for studying the structure of Xenakian sound masses, these categories are initially considered in the context of musical production. In the resulting sound masses, however, these elements interact with each other, producing constantly varying qualities at any given moment. Even though Xenakis's compositional manner is based upon the contemplation of elementary characteristics of sound, the system in production does not necessarily correspond to how the finished composition sounds. What factors, then, determine the degree of density and complexity of the sounds? And how can the Xenakian sound masses be interpreted and stratified by our ears? The present paper examines these questions through analysis of *Gmeeoorh* for organ (1974),[1] a work that contains a wide variety of sound events, from simple melody lines based upon *arborescences* to massive clusters.

Gmeeoorh is the only piece for organ by Xenakis, commissioned by the 1974 International Contemporary Organ Music Festival in Hartford.[2] According to the preface of the published score, Xenakis composed this piece with a precise image of concrete sounds, as he had been given recordings of all the stops and their range on the specific organ for which he wrote.[3] This helped him to realise

---

[1] The analysis presented in this chapter is informed by the *spectromorphological* approach originally derived from Schaeffer's concept of 'l'écoute réduite [reduced listening]' (Schaeffer 1966). The relevant bibliography includes Chion (2009), Smalley (1997) and Thoresen (2015).

[2] There exist two versions of *Gmeeoorh*, one for 61 notes and the other for 56 notes. Whilst Xenakis originally wrote the 61-note version for the Gress-Miles organ (cf. footnote 3), it is common for old organs to have a manual compass of 56 notes. It is for this reason that the composer produced the latter version – to allow the piece to be widely performed. There are only minor differences between them without any qualitative changes. In the 56-note version the beginning of the piece (bars 1-38) and the section at bars 263-273 are transposed downwards by ics 5 (perfect fourth). The purpose is simply to adjust their extremely high-pitched passages to 56-note manuals. All other sections are identical. In this chapter the 56-note version is used since the analysis relies upon the recording of Françoise Rieunier's performance on the organ at the Notre Dame de Paris (56-note compass).

[3] Gress-Miles organ in the South Congregational Church in New Britain (USA), installed in 1972.

the imaginative organ registration, which strongly characterises this piece. In order to create a rich palette of sonority, Xenakis used a variety of timbres in combination with textural writing based on linear arborescences. These unique timbres help to compensate for an inherent 'limitation' of the organ: namely the fact that it naturally produces continuous sounds with hardly any discrete impulsions. This contrasts strikingly with one of the features of Xenakis's instrumental/orchestral music – that the distinction between continuity and discontinuity plays an essential role in defining the sonic quality, as exemplified by *glissandi* and *pizzicato*. In *Gmeeoorh*, furthermore, even the typical glissandi-continuity only appears a few times as a specific effect, by sliding planks on the keyboards. Instead, a large proportion of the piece is built upon a) the fixed continuity of sustained notes and b) mobile continuity generated by textural writing of linear arborescences.

The composer notes in the preface of the score:

> *"In continuation of Erikhethon for piano and orchestra, Gmeeoorh (a free anagram of ORGANON) pursues the research of a generalisation of the melodic principle, by using linear arborescences (clonings) undergoing various transformations such as homothetic, rotations, distortions, expansions, etc..."*.

In contrast to steady solid continuity of the fixed sustained notes, the result of arborescences in *Gmeeoorh* is only an approximate continuity for two reasons. Firstly, keyboard instruments are normally framed in the twelve-note system, where intervals smaller than a semitone are not used. The most 'continuous' form in this framework is the chromatic scale, which is no more than the succession of semitone intervals. Secondly, the melodic generation by arborescences seems rather conceptual for Xenakis. As Solomos (1996, 70) comments on this issue, graphic sketching of arborescences is simply a source of imagination for the composer, and it is therefore beside the point how precisely, or even whether, the drawn outline corresponds to the resulting score and audio. In *Gmeeoorh*, the intervallic procedure is never constrained to the chromatic scale even though the outline of arborescences is represented as continual polyphonic curved lines. Aside from this discussion, the following general point should be taken into consideration for a more precise description of the organ sounds. Whilst its continuity is an approximation of transitions between pitches (musical space), organ sounds can be sustained indefinitely (musical time); there is no interruption by breath or attack, and the sounds won't naturally decay as long as the organist keeps pressing the key. In other words, notes may be connected together through legato or by overlapping preceding notes.

Approximate continuity through the use of arborescences contrasts with maximum continuity made by *glissandi*. As Xenakis often explains in his writings, *glissando* is a phenomenon of connecting two pitched notes in different temporal points with an arbitrary speed of gliding in either an upwards or downwards direction.[4] In this ceaselessly mobile sonic entity, as typically found in *Metastaesis* (1954) or *Pithoprakta* (1956), neither exact pitch nor temporal segmentation is recognised. On the other hand, the approximate continuity by arborescences consists of a number of separated pitches among which a variety of rhythmic contours can be heard. This pitch separability, or more precisely in terms of our ears' 'pitch clarity', has an essential meaning in the analysis of sound masses in *Gmeeoorh*; the pitch clarity profile – how much we can hear the individual pitches in overall texture – deeply involves the degree of density and complexity and, therefore, our aesthetic judgement of noisiness.

When most pitches are clearly heard, our attention is likely to be drawn to interval relationships either horizontally or vertically. In this case, the music is dominated by interval-centred sounds. In contrast, if pitched components are all mixed up, and the resulting sound is equal to an agglomeration with substantial density and complexity, the relationship between individual notes will not be the question. The most complex form of such an agglomerated mass would be band-forming sounds, e.g., long-sustained thick clusters. Purely interval-centred sounds and band-forming sounds thus present the two extreme points of reference in the gradation of sound density and complexity. Throughout *Gmeeoorh*, the sound goes back and forward between these two extremes, whilst flexibly changing the direction, speed and registration of linear arborescences as well as their textural interactions. In order to explore the microstructure of such varying density and complexity, we will consider the question of how the sonoristic and textural dimensions function and interact with each other in the resulting overall sound.

Analysis

1. Typology of texture, timbre, rhythm in sound masses

The degree of density and complexity clearly influences the overall structure. On the basis of the structural framework suggested by De Henau (2005), the detail of sonic formation will be examined. Exploring the internal structure that is divergent in each section, the main focus is drawn upon the following

---

[4] For example, see Xenakis (1976, 21-22).

two points: 1. the texture, which corresponds to pitch contents, rhythm and polyphonic interaction, 2. more fundamental sonic features that are relevant to our aural perception, i.e., timbre, loudness and register – all these depend upon the organ registration.

Section		Bars	Texture	Register
1	a	1–47	monophonic, interlaced	high, middle
	b	48–65	interlaced	+low
	c	66–84	layered	+low
2		85–113	band-forming clusters	full range
3		114–129	layered-hybrid	low
4	a	130–135	layered-hybrid	full range
	b	136–148	interlaced	high => middle => low
	c	149–155	layered-hybrid	full range
	d	156–195	interlaced, layered => hybrid	Variable => full range
	e	196–203	band-forming clusters (diminishing)	low
5		204–262	interval-centred	full range
6		263–274	Interlaced staccato+sustained bass	high+low
7		275–292	hybrid	full range
8		293–fine	band-forming clusters	full range

Table 3.1: **Overall structure of *Gmeeoorh***

Gmeeoorh is divided into eight sections (see Table 3.1). This segmentation derives from De Henau's analysis, which presents a comparative study of the published score with the graphic representation of arborescences from the sketch materials. In addition to this segmentation, further division can be proposed in sections 1 and 4 in terms of the texture and the sonority, as described below.

The first determinant factor to be taken into account is the polyphonic relations between the lines in the same temporal axis. In *Gmeeoorh*, there exist three basic types of texture. The piece starts with a single ascending/descending line on the Great manual, i.e., a monophonic texture, which shows the simplest form based upon interval-centred sounds (see Example 3.1). This monophonic line is eventually split-up from bar 3 and increases in textural complexity. If two or more monophonic textures are thus synchronised in a small space, also with a homogeneous timbre, the result may be an interlaced texture; individual lines are not clearly heard, but instead, as in this case, we hear a mixture of high-pitched sounds. In contrast, if there is a reasonable space or possibly heterogeneous elements between the parts, it may be heard as a layered texture. It can also be the result of several synchronised interlaced textures in different registers, whose typical example is found in section 1c. On the basis of the three types, i.e., monophonic, interlaced and layered textures, their combinations can make more complex masses, which may approach band-forming sounds. In the table, such a multiplication of basic textures is labelled as a hybrid texture.

Example 3.1: bars 1-3

Copyright 1974 © by Éditions Salabert.

The result of textural interaction largely depends upon the timbre. The melodic line may increase its quantitative density and complexity not only because of the greater number of textural lines, but also of the timbre, loudness and register. Whilst describing the timbre tends to be subjective, it *is* possible to distinguish clearly pitched sounds from ambiguous sounds comprising spectral complexity or a mixture of several pitched contents.[5] It depends, for example, upon how many partial tones are included, whether there is a subtle vibration or whether the extremities of register are used. In the case of the organ, this is relatively easy to observe since the selection of stops implies the registral and timbral characteristics. The beginning of the piece (section 1a) shows an example of an interlaced texture with massed high-pitched sounds, where all parts, even in the Pedals, share a similar sharp tone colour (see Table 3. 2). Only the Great includes the 8-foot pipes, on which high-pitched 4, 2 and 1-foot pipes are added. In the other three manuals, solid sharp sounds are made also by 4, 2 or 1-foot pipes. This homogeneity in registration and register reinforces the textural feature of the overall sound as the result of interlaced linear melodies.

---

[5] This kind of ambiguous sounds between pitched and un-pitched are defined as 'channelled [cannelé] sound' in Schaeffer's terminology; cf. Chion (2005, 166-167; original French edition 1983, 148-149).

Stratification of sound masses in Xenakis's Gmeeoorh

Great:	Rohrfl. 8'+Spitzfl. 4'+Naz. 2' $2/3$ +Waldfl. 2'+Tierce 1' $3/5$
Positive:	Blockfl. 2'+Tierce 1'$3/5$+Quintfl. 1'$1/3$+Siffl. 1'
Swell:	Oct. 1'
Pedal:	Oct. 4'+Superoct. 2'

Table 3.2: Registration in section 1

Reproduced by kind permission of Hal Leonard Europe S.r.l. – Italy.

The layered texture of section 1c (bar 66-) presents another example of registration being used to reinforce the textural formation. The chromatically ascending Pedal line starts with the *Quintaton* 16-foot stop, producing very low dull sounds whose pitches are ambiguous. The tone colour eventually becomes clearer and stronger, combining with other 16-foot stops such as the *Diapason (Principal)* or *Chimney Flute (Rohrflöte)*, as well as other high-pitched pipes, in succession (see Table 3. 3). The thick bass sound that results is entirely detached from the contrasting upper aggregate in the Great (from bar 71; joined to the high-pitched pipes of the Swell and the Positive as the result of coupler). The bars that follow also demonstrate how timbre functions in the layering process; from bar 73, the Pedal further increases in volume by successively adding strong buzzing 16-foot *Dulzian* and *Trombone (Posaune)*. This voluminous tone-colour retains its impact even when there is less difference in register; although the subsequent upper mass in the Great from bar 75 is in a lower register, the bass line can still be heard as a separated layer.

Bars 66–70		Bar 71-81
		Swell: Princip. 2'+Oct. 2'+ Quintfl. 1'$1/3$+Oct. 1'
		Positive: Oct. 2'+Blockfl. 2'+Quintfl. 1'$1/3$+ Siffl. 1'
		Great: Superoct. 2'+Waldfl. 2'
Pedal:	Quintaton 16'	
	+Princip. 16'	
	+Subbass 16'	
	+Rohrgedeckt 16'	
	+Quintfl. 10'$2/3$	
	+Superoct. 2'	
		+Basson 16'
		+Harmfl. 2'
		+Dulzian 16'
		+Posaune 16'

Table 3.3: Registration in section 1c

Reproduced by kind permission of Hal Leonard Europe S.r.l. – Italy.

After the band-forming clusters in section 2, which will be described in more detail later in this chapter, a striking shift of tone colour occurs in section 3 with the use of the *Trumpet* reed stop, which has been silent until this point (see Example 3. 2). In combination with a complex interlaced texture, this registration creates a tense mobile agglomeration, in which the movement of individual lines is hardly perceptible. In the first phrase in bars 114-116, the Great and the Positive sound in the same register (since the Great, using a 16-foot *Trumpet* stop, sounds an octave lower), and from bar 117 these two manuals are combined by coupler. Apart from those textural and timbral characteristics, a significant change of rhythm leads to an increase in density; a high degree of rhythmic consistency between the polyphonic lines results in intervallic amplifications. For example, in bars 117-118 the semiquaver rhythmic contour produces some approximately parallel movement with perfect fourths, tritones, or minor thirds. They are neither systematic nor caught by our ears. However, such vertically positioned intervals amplify the rhythmic contours, which thus serve as an important factor for constructing the thick mass. This textural manipulation is also found in bars 130-135, where the registration becomes much expanded (see Example 3. 3). The contrast between low and very high sounds is emphasised, the overall tessitura expanding to eight octaves as shown in Table 3. 4. The complex hybrid texture with a wide range comprises not only amplifications by interval as described above but also, in the bass played on the Great and the Pedal, a parallel movement at the octave, which is approximate and rhythmically unsynchronised.

Example 3.2: bars 114-118

Copyright 1974 © by Éditions Salabert.

Stratification of sound masses in Xenakis's Gmeeoorh 45

Example 3.3: bars 130-132

Copyright 1974 © by Éditions Salabert.

Swell:	Fl. oct. 4'+Viole oct. 4'+Voix cel. 4'+Princip. 2'+Oct. 2'+Tierce 1'$3/5$+Quint 1'$1/3$+Oct.1'
Positive:	Montre 8'+Holzgedeckt 8'+Princip. 4'+Rohrfl. 4'+Oct. 2'+Blockfl. 2+Tierce 1' $3/5$
Great:	Montre 16'+ Rohrgedeckt 16' + Princip. 8'+Rohrfl. 8'+Harmfl. 8'+Octave princip. 4'+Spitzfl. 4'+Grosse Tierce1'$3/5$+Superoct. 2' + Waldfl. 2'
Pedal:	Posaune 32'+Princip. 16'+Subbass 16'+Posaune 16'+Quintfl. 10' $2/3$+Basse de cornet 32'

Table 3.4: Registration in section 4, bars 131-135

Reproduced by kind permission of Hal Leonard Europe S.r.l. – Italy.

These examples demonstrate that rhythmic contours in the textural organisation affect the sound mass quality. In the process of constructing such sound masses, the function of rhythm is not to articulate time, but to exist as a stratum of sonic density. The greater the polyphonic complexity between the lines, the less likely individual components will be perceived. Our listening is instead drawn towards the rough shape, volume or direction of the overall sound rather than the detail of individual rhythms that may be masked within the interactions. Moreover, at a more fundamental level, the rhythms generated in arborescence melodies are in most cases slippery, without any metric frame of reference. Such flowing textures, especially when combined with legato playing, mean that the rhythm no longer acts as a device for dividing and systematising the time. Instead, it serves as a potential determinant of the overall density in two respects: the number of attacks filling the temporal space and the polyphonic interactions between the different lines. Whilst comparing the different sections of *Gmeeoorh*, the consequences of those rhythmic aspects will now be examined.

In relatively simple sound masses whose individual components are more or less transparent, the rhythmic cells tend to be elastic and irregular with a small number of attacks. In the opening (Example 3.1), for example, the metrical frame is blurred by the use of dotted notes or triplets, many of which are tied to the notes that follow. The contrapuntal interactions of these rhythms result in a smooth and yet unstable flow of overall texture. On the other hand, more intricate rhythms with a larger number of attacks fill the space in the complex hybrid textures as in sections 3 and 4 (see Examples 3. 2 and 3. 3). The essential point is not the detail of each rhythmic cell, which cannot be caught by our ears, but the impact of rhythmic contours upon the sound volume – supported by the synchronicity in polyphonic lines with the resulting amplification by vertical intervals, as discussed above.

In *Gmeeoorh*, the varying intricateness of rhythm seems to be carefully geared towards the overall sound quality. In section 4, different types of sound masses with wide-ranging densities are disposed in succession with kaleidoscopic changes of registration. Among the predominantly complex hybrid textures, some independent monophonic lines can be heard in the foreground of the overall mass. In order to highlight such separated lines as perceptible layers, extremely high or low registers are used, and the textures are inclined to hold simpler rhythm (e.g., the high-pitched line in the Swell in bars 152-155). In other words, the specific line is designed to be audible, detached from the stacked agglomeration. Thus, the quality of mass is also defined by the detail of rhythm and its polyphonic interaction. Whilst the detail of individual pitch or rhythm may be ultimately integrated into the mass, our ears are still sensitive not only to the resulting volume but also to the ascending/descending direction of the sound mass. Even though the transforming range and speed of arborescences are varied in each component line, inasmuch as there is a similarity in movement, especially the directional coherence, a sub-mass group can be highlighted in the complex mass. Such transparency enables us to stratify the arborescence-based masses when listening. This is exactly the point that sets these sound masses apart from the systems of sonic formation in the band-forming clusters.

2. Harmonic timbre in band-forming and interval-centred fields

The immense clusters of *Gmeeoorh* consist of fixed sustained notes filling the entire chromatic space. In order to realise such a gigantic sound in section 2, the organist is required to use four planks to press multiple notes on each of the

Stratification of sound masses in Xenakis's Gmeeoorh

three manuals and the pedals. The organist needs to gradually add stops one after another, but those additions should not be made simultaneously in the four manuals so that the additive points are not clearly spotted. As high-pitched sharp stops are successively added, the volume further increases. This technique is also applied at the end of the composition (section 8), where the maximum density of band clusters in *Gmeeoorh* is found. The organist needs to 'put on all stops and all tremulants', so that the band clusters made by the four planks with all stops drawn reach the most voluminous sound mass.

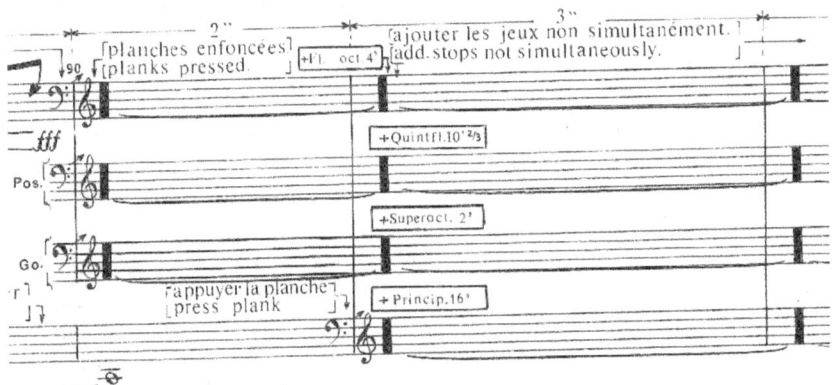

Example 3.4: Section 2, bars 90-91

Copyright 1974 © by Éditions Salabert.

What can be heard in those long-sustained blocks is mainly the property of timbre and sonic surface, which corresponds to the Schaefferian concept of *allure* defined as "the oscillation, the characteristic fluctuation in the sustainment of certain sound objects, instrumental or vocal vibrato being examples" (Chion 2005,178). Some of the organ stops have particular timbres that embrace a sort of subtle vibration, and it may even result in an effect similar to veritable iteration, such as one might find in *tremolo* or *sul ponticello*. In the case of the successive addition of stops in section 2, we hear first the fine oscillation caused by the high-register stops. As the texture subsequently comes to include stronger and low-register sounds, especially when the *Mixtures* pipes are added in bar 100, the oscillation in the sustained cluster becomes slower and clearer. This oscillation eventually leads to the tremulant in bar 102, and finally to a veritable iteration in bar 110, where the player is asked to produce "15 simultaneously but equally spaced short interruptions on all 4 planks". This example suggests that our listening focus is different in the band-forming mass. The sustained clusters draw attention to the subtlety of the sonic surface, which is not perceived in the constantly mobile texture-based masses. Indeed, in this section, the same pitch framework is sustained for more than a minute in which we hear changes in volume and timbre including *allure*. A similar effect can also be found in the sustained Pedal notes in the middle of section 4 (bars 148-51). Different stops being successively added and cancelled, the sustained notes in the bass – inserted within the complex texture-based masses – induce a sudden change in our listening focus.

The interval-centred 'chorale' in section 5 (Rieunier 1981, 241) shows the other side of extreme forms of sonic complexity. It also involves a particular manner of perception different to that of the previous example. What especially draws our attention in this section is the pitch relationship between the sustained notes. Each individual note has a strong, clear timbre, comprising both thick low sounds and sharp, high-pitched sounds (see Table 3. 5). In spite of the substantial volume of the resulting sound, the individual pitches are far more perceptible in this simple texture compared to melodic pitches generated by arborescences, especially since many notes are sustained and doubled in octaves. It is this textural formation that allows for the intervallic relations to come to the surface. The intervallic network that dominates this section relies upon tritones and open fifths (see Figure 3. 1) – sometimes replaced by perfect fourths as the inverse, or major/minor triads. Most of their shifting points are overlapped and therefore blurred. Furthermore, the 'consonant' intervals hardly appear in their purest form since they are combined with other incidental intervals. Even though major sevenths also act as important (and perceptible) intervals, as a whole, this section is framed as approximately alternating dispositions of tritones and fifths. Thus in the successive appearance of the intensified intervals mentioned above, we can hear a reference to the dynamic between consonance and dissonance.

Swell:	Princip. 2'+Tierce 1'$3/5$+Zembelstern 1'$1/3$+ Quintfl. 10' $1/3$+Oct. 1'
Positive:	Gedecktpommer 16'+Dulzian 16'+Tromp. 8'+Cornet 8'+Fl. à cheminee 8'+ Rohrfl. 4'+Oct. 2+ Naz. 2' $2/3$+Tierce 1'$3/5$+Blockfl. 2'
Great:	Tromp. à pavillon 8'+Clarion à pavillon 4'
Pedal:	Subbass 16'+Quintfl. 10' $2/3$+Basson 16'

Table 3.5: Registration in section 5, bars 204-252

Reproduced by kind permission of Hal Leonard Europe S.r.l. – Italy.

Stratification of sound masses in Xenakis's Gmeeoorh   49

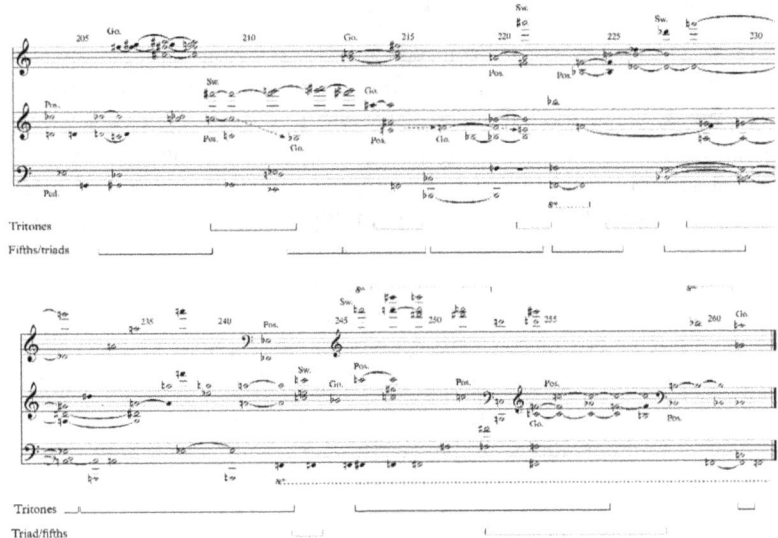

Figure 3.1: Harmonic reduction of section 5 with the remarks of dominant interval relationships

According to aural analysis by the present author, acoustically 'hidden' notes are omitted in this example. In the light of their registration, the Swell and the Pedal are notated in actual registers as heard, i.e., two octaves higher for the former and an octave lower for the latter compared to the notes in the published score.

Tritones and open fifths take precedence in this section and this homogeneity bestows a kind of intervallic logic to this passage. Those intervallic relationships are clearly perceived due to the long-sustained durations, in sharp distinction to instances of unstable mobile masses. To sum up, neither agglomeration nor a 'crash' of heterogeneities is found in this sonic field. When the number of heterogeneous elements exceeds our ability to hear the individual sonorities and their relationships, the sound mass tends to exhibit a certain noisiness. As we have discussed, polyphonic complexity and textural density mostly correspond to a degree of noisiness. But this is only the case when the music is perceived by our ears as being non-intervallic. This argument certainly should not be confused with interval logic in the process of composition. Even when the overall sound consists of a quantitatively dense texture, as long as it is built in a homogeneous framework of intervals, the level of noisiness will not approach band-forming sounds in our perception.

Conclusion

Band-forming masses, interval-centred sounds and various masses in-between, as the result of heterogeneous polyphonic interaction: such different structures bring diversity to the organ sound in *Gmeeoorh*. It is the dynamic between these structures that give rise to the entire form of the piece. The linear arborescences, which start with a single melody, increase in their interactive complexity throughout section 1. In parallel to the multiplication of textural writing, the range of register and timbre becomes gradually wider. The growth of complexity in the mobile masses is nevertheless neutralised in section 2, by a sudden move to thick sustained clusters. Section 3 reopens the arborescence formation but now in a more dynamic way. Register, loudness, timbre and the textural interaction frequently change, which results in a succession of many different masses: e.g., soft-tone interlaced textures with a small range of register, voluminous agglomerations or layered textures with an enormous gap in register. Such an assortment of masses eventually leads to the interval-centred section 5, in which the density in the overall sound is 'reduced' to a homogeneous network of intervallic relationships. This minimal level of complexity contrasts with the final amplification at section 7, which is transitioned to in section 6 with light staccato articulation and the long-sustained bass. The maximum level of band-forming clusters is finally reached in section 8, which is even stronger than in section 2, to close the piece.

In this chapter, sound density and complexity are described as the interactive result of texture and more elementary sonic features such as register, loudness and timbre. The analysis of *Gmeeoorh* presented here clarifies the structure of mass formation processes, i.e., the stratification of sound quality as follows:

1. Register, loudness, timbre.

2. Textural quantity: the number of pitches, rhythmic density (the speed of rhythmic contours).

3. Textural quality: proportion of homogeneity/heterogeneity, rhythmic or intervallic consistency, direction of sound procedure, spatial distance.

Most of the factors are certainly linked to the categories mentioned by Xenakis (cited at the beginning of this paper), and the 'proportion of homogeneity/heterogeneity' probably coincides with what he calls "degree of order". However, it is not only in the composer's sonic construction (poiesis) that these three strata serve as important factors; they are also pertinent to our reception. In order to understand the structure of sound masses, in addition, the power balance between their interactions needs to be considered. Combining some heterogeneous elements in the same mass requires a well-balanced proportion of subsonic groups. Thanks to subtle manipulations of many different elements, the overall sound can be diversified into foreground and background structures even in highly complex masses. In this sense, the dynamic between the homogeneity and the heterogeneity in sonic microstructures provides an essential approach to our understanding of the diversity of Xenakis's sonic universe.

Bibliography

Chion, Michel. 2009. *Guide to Sound Objects*, translated by John Dack and Christine North. https://monoskop.org/File:Chion_Michel_Guide_To_Sound_Objects_Pierre_Schaeffer_and Musical_Research.pdf. (Accessed 20 October 2017). Originally published in French as *Guide des objets sonores: Pierre Scaheffer et la recherche musicale*, Paris: Buchet-Chastel, 1983.

De Henau, Joris. 2005. "*Gmeeoorh* (1974) for Organ by Iannis Xenakis: Towards a Critique of the Arborescence." In *International Symposium, Iannis Xenakis: Conference Proceedings. Athens, Greece, 18-20 May 2005*, edited by Anastasia Georgaki and Makis Solomos. National and Kapodistrian University of Athens, School of philosophy, Music Department; University of Montpellier 3, 150-160.

Rieunier, Françoise. 1981. "Sur *Gmeeoorh*." In *Regards sur Iannis Xenakis*, edited by Hugues Gerhards. Paris: Stock.

Schaeffer, Pierre. 1966. *Traité des objets musicaux*. Paris: Seuil.

Smalley, Denis. 1997. "Spectromorphology: Explaining Sound-Shapes", *Organised Sound* 2 (2): 107–126.

Solomos, Makis. 1996. *Iannis Xenakis*. Mercurès: P.O. Edition.

Thoresen, Lasse. 2015. *Emergent Musical Forms. Aural Explorations*. London, ON: Department of Music, Research and Composition, Univeristy of Western Ontario.

Xenakis, Iannis. 1976. *Musique. Artchitecture*. 2nd edn, revised and augmented. Tounai: Casterman.

Xenakis, Iannis. 1992. *Formalized Music: Thought and Mathematics in Composition*, edited by Sharon Kanach. New York: Pendragon Press.

Discography

Rieunier, Françoise, 2001. *Xenakis/Chaynes/Chapelet: L'Orgue contemporain à Notre-Dame de Paris* [CD], France, Disques du Solstice, SOCD 192.

Chapter 4

On *Herma*

Benoît Gibson

Iannis Xenakis's *Herma*, for piano solo, was composed in 1960-61 and premiered in 1962, in Tokyo, by Yuji Takahashi, to whom the work is dedicated. According to the composer, *Herma* means 'bond' but also 'foundation' or 'embryo', etc. Relying on documents consulted in the Xenakis Archives,[1] the aim of this article is to provide new insights into how Xenakis conceived his first piano work. It shows the relationship between *Herma* and one of the composer's earlier pieces, *Achorripsis*, and offers a new understanding of what may have caused some of the discrepancies between the theory on which *Herma* is based and its application in the score.

Classes of pitches

It is well known that some aspects of *Herma* are based on the definition of four classes of pitches (R, A, B, C) and the logical operations imposed upon them. Class R comprises all the keys of the piano, of which the three classes A, B and C form subsets of 24, 21 and 25 notes respectively (Figure 1). Xenakis does not specify how the classes were defined, except for class R. The choice of the individual notes within the classes A, B and C may have been influenced by the sonority they create.

In the sketches reproducing *Herma*'s classes of pitches, there are numbers added above or below some of the notes (OM[2] 12-29). These numbers do not represent intervals, densities or occurrences of pitches. They are fingerings! The ones below the stave are the fingerings for the left hand; those above the stave, for the right. Why would Xenakis add fingerings to some of the classes of pitches in his sketches? Fingerings are inside-time, and there are no

---

[1] I am grateful to Mâkhi Xenakis for allowing me to consult the documents related to *Herma* in the Xenakis Archives.
[2] OM stands for 'Œuvres Musicales' [Musical Works], and refers to files in the Xenakis Archives.

passages in *Herma* that require conjunct motion or lines of adjacent notes. We can easily imagine Xenakis playing *Herma*'s classes of pitches as scales, or sieves, as he would call them later. Adding fingerings would make it easier for him to play as a way to hear the sonority of the sound created. As Helffer (2010, 106) remarks: 'in the end, and contrary to Boulez for instance, Xenakis does not have an analytical ear; he is much more sensitive to resonance'.

Structure

From a compositional point of view, *Herma* falls into three sections. The first (bars 1-29) is based on the pitches of class R and features a progressive increase of dynamic and density. On an early sketch of the first section (OM 12-29, 3), Xenakis pencilled in the word 'inondation?' ['inundation?'] in French, conveying the idea that the music should become progressively overwhelming. He imagined the increase of density by maintaining the same number of sounds (26) while reducing the length of each sequence by the golden ratio (0.618): 15", 9.30", 5.73", 3.54", 2.20", 1.35", 0.83", 0.51", 0.32". In the temporal flow chart of *Herma*, the corresponding densities are figured in sounds per second: 1.73, 2.80, 4.53, 7.32, 11.8, 19, 31 (Xenakis 1992, 177).

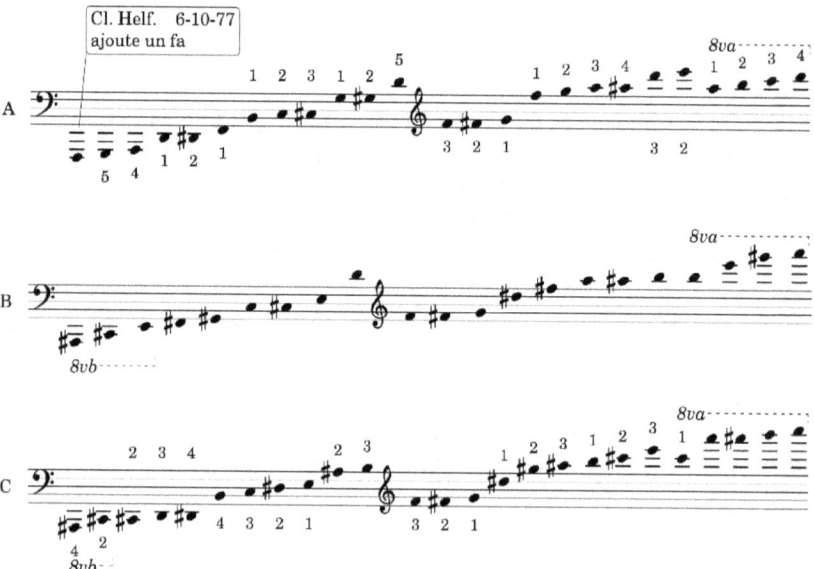

Figure 4.1: *Herma*: classes *A*, *B* and *C*

On Herma

In the second section (bars 30-135), which is sometimes referred to as 'Exposition', we hear pitches from classes A, B and C, each one followed by its negation (the pitches that do not belong to A, B or C): $\overline{A}, \overline{B}, \overline{C}$. Two sketches related to this section bear the indication 'Algebra' (OM 12-27, 1 and OM 12-19, 3). The third section (bars 136-219) applies further logical operations upon the classes of pitches A, B, C and their negation: union and intersection.[3] Figure 2, drawn after Xenakis's own sketch (1992, 176), displays the order in which the new classes appear in the score. They are organised in two planes, each one divided into two dynamic levels. Both planes converge towards the last class, F, which Xenakis represents by two different expressions according to the number of operations implied (1992, 173):

$$F = ABC + \overline{AB}C + \overline{ABC} + A\overline{BC} \quad (1)$$

$$F = (AB + \overline{AB})C + \overline{(AB + \overline{AB})C} \quad (2)$$

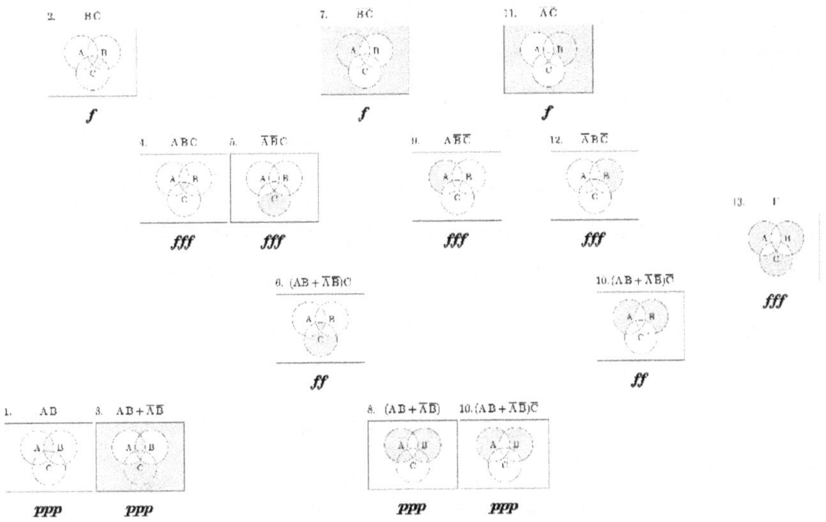

Figure 4.2: *Herma*: flow chart of bars 136-219

---

[3] Union is symbolised by a plus sign (+); intersection by juxtaposition.

Graphic representation

With the exception of the first section,[4] Xenakis also represented *Herma* graphically, in a pitch versus time domain, before transcribing it into traditional notation. Figure 3 is a graphic representation that corresponds to excerpts from the second section of *Herma*. Xenakis indicates the pitches of class *A* on the left-hand side of the graph as reference points. But, contrary to what would be usual, he writes the different layers on different pages, as if different parts were written separately, similar to what composers would do before the invention of the score. What is even more surprising, is that when Xenakis reaches the end of the page, he goes back to its beginning and continues with a different colour, instead of using another page.[5] And he does this twice. This means that the graphic representation reproduced in Figure 3 does not correspond to the score, but to the superimposition of three layers that appear successively in *Herma*. It represents only the pitches of class *A* played *ff* with a density of 0.8 sounds per second. The other layer, which also features class *A* but played *pp* successively with a density of 3.3 and 5 sounds per second, is written on other pages. To some extent, this demonstrates that, at least initially, Xenakis conceived the different layers of *Herma* separately, as independent clouds of sounds.

The graphic representation is the ultimate stage of the compositional process before transcribing the data into traditional notation, where Xenakis still has to choose the duration of the individual sounds and add the indications of pedalling. The sketch reproduced in Figure 3 starts at zero second, which indicates a beginning. Could it be that, at the time when Xenakis started composing his first piano piece, he did not have the idea of classes of pitches in mind, and that the first section of *Herma* was added afterwards? That could explain the different titles, 'inondation' and 'Algebra', and why some of the pitches of class *R* are not heard.

Stochastic distributions

There is a similarity in the way Xenakis composed the first section of *Herma* and *Achorripsis* (1957) for 21 instruments. The latter relies on the stochastic distribution of seven sonic events, each one associated with a group of

---

[4] To my knowledge, there is no graphic representation of bars 1-29 of *Herma* in the Xenakis Archives.
[5] In the original sketch (OM 12-19, 23), Xenakis uses colours and not symbols to differentiate the three subdivisions notated in seconds: grey (0-24 sec.), green (25-49 sec.) and red (50-60 sec.).

instruments or their playing techniques. We know from his writings that Xenakis (1992, 29-37) calculated the probability of occurrences of these sonic events using the Poisson distribution (which is the law of appearance of rare random events), and that he represented them by a matrix where each line corresponds to a 'timbre' and each column to a unit of time (of 6.5 bars). Xenakis also used other formulas to calculate the probabilities of occurrences of durations and intervals within each sonic event. In *Herma*, like in *Achorripsis*, the tables representing distributions of durations and intervals only provide global proportions of numbers without prescribing any order. They are outside-time. This is probably why Xenakis also represented them linearly, in lexicographic time, as classes of durations and intervals before transcribing them into traditional notation.

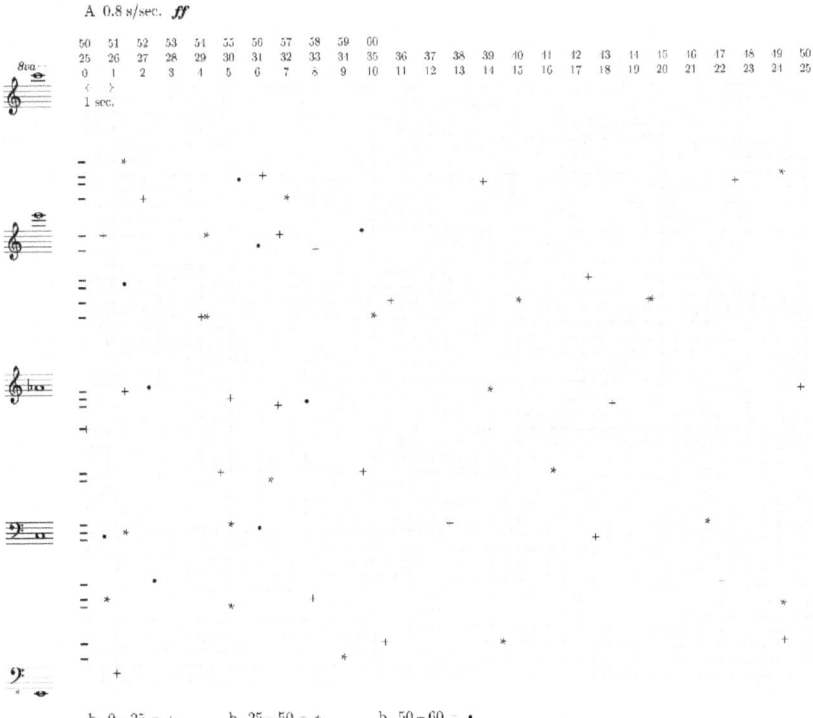

Figure 4.3: *Herma*: graphic representations of class *A*, *ff*, 0.8 sounds/sec

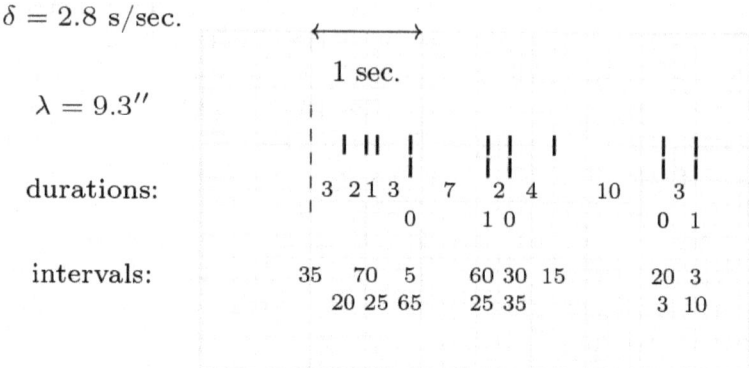

Figure 4.4: *Herma*, bars 7-8: classes of durations and intervals

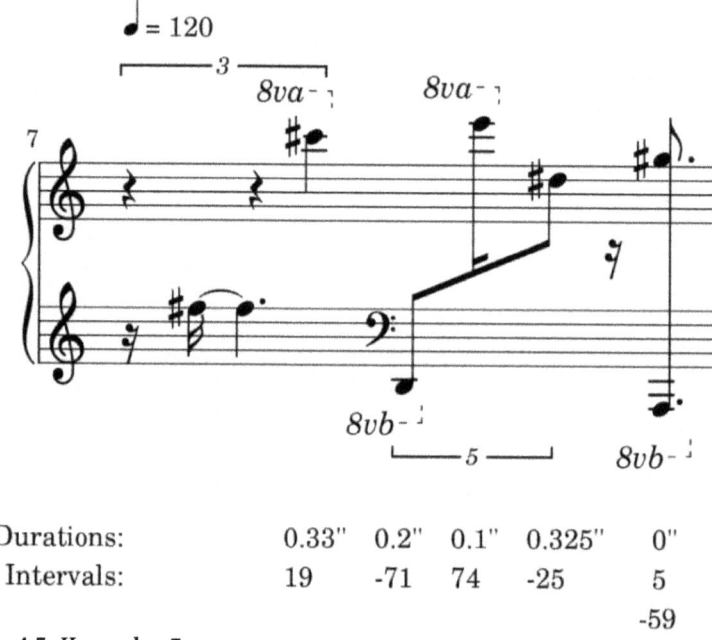

Figure 4.5: *Herma*, bar 7

Figure 4 is a transcription drawn following a document found in the Xenakis Archives (OM 12-19, 3). Classes of intervals and durations are written out below the marks corresponding to the attacks of the notes. This is an intermediate stage in the compositional process. It leaves the composer with many subjective choices. Melodic intervals, which can be ascending or descending, are represented as multiple of five semitones;[6] and durations, as tenths of a second. The data displayed in Figure 4 correspond to bar 7 of *Herma* (Figure 5).

In the preface to the score of *Herma*,[7] Xenakis explains that 'The elements of each class are presented stochastically, that is unrestrictedly, in order not to disturb the basic plan of operations and of logical relationship between classes'. A close analysis of the piece reveals that Xenakis did not calculate all the stochastic distributions. He borrowed them from earlier work(s). At least some of the durations and densities of *Herma* are derived from *Achorripsis*. Xenakis numbered the columns of the original matrix of *Achorripsis* using an ancient Greek alphabetic numeral system (Xenakis 1992, 28). In the graphic score of *Herma* (OM 12-19), there are references to these numbers without referring explicitly to *Achorripsis*. The graphic representation of the first occurrence of class *C*, for instance, is accompanied with the indication ιζ'-VII (OM12-19, 10), which corresponds to the 'String arco' sonic event of bars 104-110 of *Achorripsis*. Figure 6 compares graphic representations of *Achorripsis* and *Herma*. In the graphic score of *Achorripsis* (a), Xenakis indicates the instruments (V, VC, CB), the timbre, or sonic event (string arco, played *f*) and the subdivision of the minim (3, 4, 5).[8] The comparison shows that Xenakis transposed the pitches of *Achorripsis* to the closest pitches of class *C* and adapted the durations in order to fit a subdivision of the beat by 5. A more detailed analysis of the relationship between *Herma* and *Achorripsis* would also demonstrate that Xenakis treated some excerpts in retrograde forms, as was his common practice when borrowing excerpts from earlier works (Gibson 2011, 21).

---

[6] Xenakis replaced 0 by 3.
[7] Boosey & Hawkes, 1967.
[8] The numbers 3, 4 and 5 before each instrument indicate the subdivision of the beat on which the sound fall.

Figure 4.6: Comparison between graphic representations of *Achorripsis* and *Herma*
Achorripsis, String arco, bars 104-105 (left); *Herma*, bars 160-161 (right).

Edition(s) of the score

Herma was first commercially published by Boosey & Hawkes in 1967. Until then, the score existed as a facsimile of the composer's autograph. In a prior publication (Gibson 1994), I referred to the existence of two different printed editions of *Herma*. At the time, my claim was that not all of the discrepancies found in Xenakis's scores were motivated by aesthetic reasons. Some are what we can call errors, or, at least, unintentional choices. The 1978 reprint edition of *Herma* supported my claim by correcting some of the discrepancies. Claude Helffer (2010, 105), who also claimed that 'the first editions of *Herma* were full of errors', is likely to have been responsible for correcting the score.[9] In the sketch of class *A* reproduced in Figure 1, a pencilled annotation reads: 'Cl. Helf 6-10-77 ajoute un fa' [Claude Helffer, 6th October 1977, adds an F]. The F1 added to class *A* appears in bar 30. Theoretically, F1 doesn't belong to class *A* and should have been notated an octave higher. This is where it appears in the graphic representation of that layer (OM 12-19, 23). But it is one of the few moments where the pitches are easily recognisable in *Herma*. And by that time, the piece had been performed many times. It probably appeared to Helffer as a better solution to leave that note as it is and change the one that belongs to the negation of class *A* ($\bar{A}$). This is one of the alterations found in the 1978 reprint edition (bar 64): the original F1 is changed to F♯1. But Helffer did not carry on and alter the other classes of pitches that result from the application of logical operations. For instance, if class *A* includes an F1, then so should class $A\,\bar{B}\,\bar{C}$, and no F1 was added to class $A\,\bar{B}\,\bar{C}$. In fact, Helffer's corrections only concern the first twelve pages of the score.

Figure 4.7: *Herma*: Discrepancies of pitches in classes *A* and $\bar{A}$

---

[9] There is an annotated printed score of *Herma* in the Xenakis Archives that bears the note: 'Cl. Helffer / Corrigé [Corrected] le 8-11-72'.

Many scholars have studied the discrepancies between the theory put forward by Xenakis and its realisation in the score. Figure 7 compares the number of occurrences of common pitches found in classes A and $\overline{A}$, as calculated by Bayer (1981), Montague (1995) and Wannamaker (2001), together with the corresponding pitches in the 1978 reprint edition of the score and how these pitches were notated in the graphic representation of *Herma* (OM 12-19). The fact that scholars don't reach exactly the same numbers may be symptomatic of the difficulty of carrying out a task easily prone to error. The 1978 reprint edition corrected all but five of the discrepancies found between class A and its negation.[10] It is noticeable that, except for a few added *ottava* signs, in most cases, Helffer opted for the closest pitch within the class indicated in the score. It seems logical to proceed that way if one relies only on the original classes of pitches. But a close examination of the graphic score of *Herma* (OM 12-19) provides a different understanding of what may have caused the discrepancies found in the score. Of the 10 corrected errors of classes A and $\overline{A}$, only one matches the corresponding pitch in the graphic score: B1 (bar 70). We could carry on the comparison with the graphic score and verify that, in the $\overline{C}$ section, Xenakis omitted the d♯ of class C notated on the left-hand side of the page (OM12-19, 20), which didn't prevent him from using that pitch. Later, the 1978 reprint edition of *Herma* corrected all but one, the e♭ in bar 128.

Other discrepancies resulted from transpositions. It appears that Xenakis transposed the first occurrences of class $(\overline{AB} + \overline{AB})\overline{C}$ 2 semitones down. We find the same kind of deviation with class $\overline{A}\,\overline{C}$, but transposed 4 semitones up. Finally, there are also pitches that belong to the classes indicated above, but are deviations in relation to the graphic score.

There should be no doubt that Xenakis wanted the score to be corrected, as is made clear in the following two quotes from the composer's correspondence. The first one is extracted from a letter from Xenakis to Helen S. Walker,[11] dated 11 January 1976, about the apparent departures from a literal application of the classes and operations in *Herma*:

---

[10] The 1978 reprint edition of *Herma* incorporated forty-one of the forty-four pitch corrections that Helffer provided to Rosalie La Grow Sward (1981, 573-574).

[11] Helen S. Walker introduced herself to Xenakis as a doctoral student in piano pedagogy at the University of Colorado.

"[T]he departure from the original sets of pitches are due to random errors of mine or of the cop[y]ist. They are gradually corrected in the successive editions of the score."[12]

The second one, which provides an even more telling argument, is an excerpt from a letter of 8th May 1969 from Xenakis to Rufina Ampenoff of Boosey & Hawkes:

"You remember the case of Herma. Last week, I was invited to the Oberlin College as a guest composer where I gave 3 conferences 1) to musicians 2) to mathem[aticians] 3) to architects and where Morsima-Amorsima, Atrées, Polla ta Dhina and Herma were played. On the occasion of my visit, the teachers analysed Herma for their students and discovered the errors! They must be corrected in the next reprint.[13]" (Boosey & Hawkes Archive, uncatalogued material held at the British Library)

The question of the criteria on which the corrections should be based remains. One could imagine a revised edition that would take as a starting point not the original classes of pitches, but the graphic representation of *Herma*.

Recordings

Herma stands as one of Xenakis's most recorded pieces. Figure 8 lists 16 commercially issued recordings of the work, together with information about performer, year of release, edition of the score, duration and label. They fall into two groups separated by 14 years (1968-1977 and 1991-2018). The first six were originally released on LP. Among these, four were later made available on CD. At the time of this writing, the ones marked with an asterisk (*) (Yuji Takahashi's first recording and the one by Jacqueline Méfano) are only available on LP.

---

[12] Cited in Solomos (2013).
[13] "*Vous vous souvenez du cas Herma. La semaine dernière j'ai été invité au Oberlin College as a guest composer ou j'ai donné 3 conférences 1) aux musiciens 2) aux mathém. 3) au architectes et où on a joué Morsima-Amorsima, Atrées, Polla ta Dhina et Herma. Or à l'occasion de ma venue les prof. ont analysé la pièce Herma à leurs élèves et on découvert les fautes! Il faut absolument au prochain tirage les corriger.*"

Performer	Year	Edition	Duration	Label
George Pludermacher	1968	1967	7:59	EMI Classics 6 87674 2
Yuji Takahashi	1970	1967	6:43	MAINSTREAM Records – MS/5000*
Jacqueline Méfano	1971	1967	8:14	DISQUES ADÈS - 16.005*
Aki Takahashi	1973	1967	6:53	EMI QIAG-50035-37
Yuji Takahashi	1976	1967	7:25	DENON 33CO-1052
Geoffrey Madge	1977	1967	7:25	BVHAAST CD 0706
Claude Helffer	1991	1978	7:11	MONTAIGNE 782005
Stephanie McCallum	1993	1967	9:44	TALL POPPIES TP037
Ermis Theodorakis	1996	1967	13:21	ATHENS MUSIC SOCIETY
Justin Rubin	1997	1978	7:48	VANDENBURG VAN 0003
Aki Takahashi	1999	1967	7:38	MODE 80
Leon Michener	2002	1978	7:23	FMR CD95-C06
Marc Ponthus	2003	1967	8:34	NEUMA 450-104
[Daniel Grossmann]	2008	1967	6:36	NEOS 10707
Stéphanos Thomopoulos	2010	1978	10:03	TIMPANI - 1C 1232
David Ezra Okonşar	2016	1967	10:51	LMO Records 2016-22-12

Figure 4.8: Commercially issued recordings of *Herma*

Of all these recordings, only four were made from a score that includes the pitch corrections found in the 1978 reprint edition of *Herma*. As for duration, most performers who took up the challenge of recording *Herma* played the work at a slower tempo than the one notated in the score[14] – on paper, *Herma* has a duration of circa 6:40. One recalls Xenakis's comment about Helffer's tempo:

> "One day, I played Herma at the radio. When Xenakis heard that recording, he told me my tempo was too fast. I verified the indications on the score and my timing was accurate down to the second. I told him so. His response: 'Make your seconds last longer!'" (Helffer 2010, 106)

How much longer should the seconds be? Yuji Takahashi told Xenakis that *Herma* was playable, or more accurately, 'not impossible' (Varga 1995, 40), which is not the case of all of Xenakis's piano music. In order to make the piece more or less playable, performers adapt their tempo. The average tempos of the recordings listed in Figure 8 vary considerably. Theodorakis's recording, for instance, features an average tempo twice as slow as the prescribed one, thus showing a great concern with playing all the notes. But close listening to the recordings also reveals that very often performers omit

---

[14] Durations are measured up from the onset of the first note to the end of the piece, including the resonance of the last notes.

notes, mis-hit others or change octaves. Helffer refers to the performance of *Herma* as a process of successive approximations:

> *"I believe that even at 80% [of what is written], a performer is able to transmit an accurate idea of the work's global sound."* (Helffer 2010, 101)

What is meant by what is written? Playing all the notes? This seems to be the idea behind the following quote from the liner notes for NEOS's release of Xenakis's music for keyboard instruments realised by computer:

> *"The desire to hear a composition exactly as Xenakis had in all probability imagined it – the notation is precise enough – remains legitimate nevertheless. The conductor Daniel Grossmann presents with this CD possibly the first attempt at a reconstruction of the aural imaginings of the composer."* (Tom Sora, CD NEOS 10707)

It is highly questionable whether the final result on this CD corresponds to the aural imaginings of the composer. When referring to *Herma*, scholars and performers have sometimes put much if not all the emphasis on pitches – and Xenakis is partly responsible for that. But *Herma* is also, and one could argue, mainly, about contrasts, contrasts of dynamics, densities and resonance between clouds of sounds. Finding the right balance between independent layers of sounds is one of *Herma*'s most challenging features. In the performing notes to the score of *Synaphai* (1969)[15] for piano and orchestra, one reads: 'The pianist plays all the lines, if he can'. To paraphrase Xenakis, one could say about *Herma*: The pianist plays all the dynamics and densities, if he can!

Bibliography

Bayer, Francis. 1981. *De Schönberg à Cage. Essai sur la notion d'espace sonore dans la musique contemporaine*. Paris: Klincksieck.

Gibson, Benoît. 1994. "La théorie et l'œuvre chez Xenakis: éléments pour une réflexion". *Circuit. Revue Nord-Américaine de Musique du XXe Siècle*, 5 (2): 41-54.

Gibson, Benoît. 2011. *The Instrumental Music of Iannis Xenakis. Theory, Practice, Self-borrowing*, Hillsdale: Pendragon.

Helffer, Claude. 2010. "On *Herma, Erikhthon*, and others". In *Performing Xenakis*, edited by Sharon Kanach. Hillsdale: Pendragon, 99-114.

Montague, Eugene. 1995. "The limits of logic: structure and aesthetics in Xenakis's *Herma*". *Ex Tempore*, 7 (2): 36-65.

---

[15] Éditions Salabert, 1985.

Solomos, Makis. 2013. "Iannis Xenakis. Trois composantes de l'univers xénakien." In *Théories de la composition musicale au XXe siècle*, edited by Nicolas Donin and Laurent Feneyrou. Lyon: Symétrie, 2, 1057-1080.

Sward, Rosalie la Grow. 1981. *An Examination of the Mathematical Systems used in Selected Compositions of Milton and Iannis Xenakis*. Northwestern University: PhD.

Varga, Bálint András. 1996. *Conversations with Iannis Xenakis*. London: Faber and Faber.

Wannamaker, Robert A. 2001. "Structure and perception in *Herma* by Iannis Xenakis." *Music Theory Online*, 7 (3). Available at http://mto.societymusic theory.org/issues/mto.01.7.3/ toc.7.3.html (Accessed 2 July 2018).

Xenakis, Iannis. 1992. *Formalized Music. Thought and Mathematics in Composition*. Stuyvesant: Pendragon.

Part III - Performance

Chapter 5

Performances in Iannis Xenakis's electroacoustic music

Reinhold Friedl

It is widely known that Xenakis used instrumental recordings in his electroacoustic compositions. He did this in multifaceted ways – in his first compositions for tape in the late 1950s Xenakis used to compose his basic sound material: he recorded basic sounds like a bell or glowing coal. He then transposed these sounds, combined and densified them, often to build up complex textures. This technique can be found in *Diamorphoses* (1957), *Concret PH* (1958) and *Analogiques B* (1959).

In the early 1960s Pierre Schaeffer, the head of the *Groupe de Recherches Musicales* (GRM) in Paris, succeeded to obtain some film music commissions for the members of the group. Xenakis composed three soundtracks: *Orient Occident* (1960), *Vasarely* (1960, withdrawn), and *Formes rouges* (1961, withdrawn). Two of them, *Vasarely* and *Form rouges*, have been instrumental pieces recorded on tape and have been subsequently withdrawn. The film music for *Orient Occident* was shortened from about 17 minutes to less than 11 minutes by cutting out mostly instrumental passages. In 1962 Xenakis composed *Bohor* and used instrumental sound sources, which will be discussed in detail in this article. Xenakis then started to record musical material especially composed for his electroacoustic music, as, e.g., full orchestra scores: *Polytope de Montreal* (1967, prerecorded orchestra), *Kraanerg* (1969, orchestra and tape) and *Hibiki-Hana-Ma* (1970, prerecorded orchestra). The following compositions for multimedia projects, his so-called *Polytopes*, combine all kind of different prerecorded acoustic materials, including instrumental sounds: *Persepolis* (1971), *Polytope de Cluny* (1972) and first electronic sounds in *La Légende d'Eer (Diatope)* (1977). With the next piece *Mycènae Alpha (Polytope de Mycène)* (1978), Xenakis reduced his sound material more and more to electronically generated sounds, produced in his new research center in Paris CeMaMu (Centre d'études de mathématique et automatique musicales, founded in 1972).

This article focuses on two pieces: *Bohor*, the first electroacoustic composition with large instrumental parts, and *La Légende d'Eer*, the last multi-channel piece. What kinds of instrumental sounds have been used in these pieces? Are they just prerecorded sounds, improvisations or performances?

The results presented here for the first time are findings of my PhD project 'Philology of Electroacoustic Music' at Goldsmiths, University of London.[1] These would have been impossible without access to digitized audio tapes, scores, drafts, notebooks, and other paper-based sources in the following archives: Xenakis Archive at Bibliothèque Nationale de France, BnF, Paris; Private archive of the Xenakis family, Paris; Archiv des Westdeutschen Rundfunks WDR Köln, Germany; Archives of the edition house Durant-Salabert-Eschig, Paris; Archives of INA/GRM, Radio France, Paris.[2]

Bohor (1962)

Bohor was premiered in Paris, Salle des Conservatoires on December 15, 1962. It is remarkable that there is only one source referring to that date: the *Répertoire acousmatique*. (INA-GRM, 1980). Benoît Gibson underlines that even Maurice Fleuret, who was an important supporter of Xenakis's work, did not mention the concert in an article from December 27, 1962 (Fleuret 1962 cited in Gibson 2015). Fleuret mentions *ST 10*, a chamber music composition by Xenakis, as part of 'the last concert of the GRM'. Gibson points out that ST 10 had already been premiered in May 1962. *Bohor*, just performed in a GRM concert a few days before the article was released, is not mentioned. Till today it was not clear whether *Bohor* was played in this concert or not, or even whether this concert took place. In 2018, I was able to obtain a scan of the concert programme that still exists at the Groupe de Recherches Musicales in Paris.[3] It proves that *Bohor* was performed on December 15, 1962, and *ST10* has been performed in a concert on December 19, 1962. It remains astonishing that the performance of *Bohor* in 1962 has not been mentioned,

---

[1] I thank Goldsmiths, University of London for the generous support of my participation in the Symposium 'Exploring Xenakis: Performance, Practice, Philosophy', University of Leeds 2017.

[2] This research would not have been possible without generous support and help by Françoise and Mâkhi Xenakis, Frank Hilberg (WDR Köln), Volker Müller (WDR Köln Studio für elektronische Musik), Katja Teubner (Audiosuite Köln), Makis Solomos (Université Paris 8), Pascal Cordereix (BnF), Eric Denut and Patricia Alia (Durand-Salabert-Eschig), Yann Geslin, Evélyne Gayou and Daniel Teruggi (GRM).

[3] Many thanks to François Bonnet, directeur du GRM Paris.

but the performance in 1968 was regarded as the 'biggest scandal' (Chion, 1972) in the history of electroacoustic music.

Several texts and analyses of *Bohor* have been published, but only decades later.[4] The only earlier text can be found on the LP *Iannis Xenakis Electroacoustic Music*, released in 1970 by Nonesuch (Xenakis 1970). James Mansback Brody's liner notes contain important references/valuable information. It can be assumed that Brody discussed the liner notes with the composer: at that time Brody was Xenakis's composition student at Bloomington University, where Xenakis held a teaching position from 1967 to 1972.

Bohor is listed in the GRM catalogue (INA-GRM 1980, 285; Gayou 2007, 373) as the first 8-track composition at the GRM. But 8-track did not mean that the final composition was realised on an 8-track-tape. The first 8-track-machine arrived at GRM only in 1977 (Gayou 2007, 373). In fact, Xenakis used 4 Stereo-tape-machines for Bohor, so 4 x 2 = 8 tracks, and the complete production process was realised on stereo tapes. First, Xenakis recorded sound materials. Evelyne Gayou points out that those recordings have probably been the first stereo recordings made at GRM. The first stereo tape machine had arrived at GRM in 1958 (INA-GRM 1980, 285). Xenakis called the final four stereo tracks – derived somehow from those recordings – 'piano', 'orgue', 'irak' and 'byzance'. All articles discussing the sound material (Harley 2002, Kim and Berissov 2004, Couprie 2006. Hünermann 2009, Gibson 2015) come to the conclusion that 'piano' stands for 'prepared piano', and that 'orgue' stands for a transposed mouth organ from Laos. 'Irak' is interpreted as the sound of jewelry and/or small percussion instruments from Irak. 'Byzance' has been associated with the sound of jewelry and bracelets, too.

In the drafts and notes at the Xenakis Archives (OM 33-11) the following names (and no others) are used for the final eight tracks:

Table 1

	track		abbreviation
Tape I	1	Piano	pi
	2	Piano	pi
Tape II	3	Orgue	org
	4	Orgue	org

---

[4] Harley 2002; Harley 2004; Kim and Borissov 2004; Couprie 2006; Hünermann 2009; Gibson, 2015; Turner 2015.

Tape III	5	Byzance	By
	6	Byzance	By
Tape IV	7	Irak	ir
	8	Irak	ir

Xenakis used the same names in his mixing schemes and drafts:

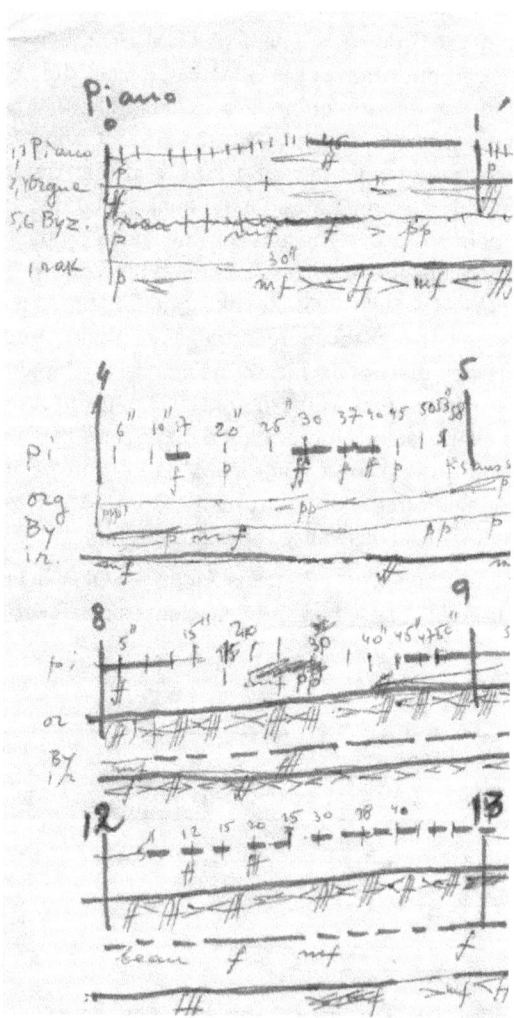

Figure 5.1: *Bohor*, **scheme probably for mix-down or performance**
Detail of OM 33-11-p10 (Archives Xenakis P), Original ca 29 cm x 21 cm, 1986 or earlier.

Performances in Iannis Xenakis's electroacoustic music 73

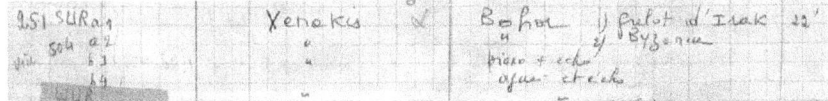

Figure 5.2: Names of the 4 stereo tracks of *Bohor*
Registre des Originaux (INA-GRM a), 251 SUR.

The tapes in the GRM archives are listed in the *Registre des Originaux* (INA-GRM a, no date) as follows:

Table 2

251 SUR	a1	Bohor, 1) Grelot d'Irak
	a2	Bohor 2) Byzance
	b3	piano + echo
	b4	orgue et écho

In the GRM Excel file (INA-GRM b, no date), they are named:

Table 3

251 SUR a	1/	a 1) Grelot d'Irak
	2/	2) Byzance
251 SUR b	1/	b 3) plan 0 + echo
	2/	4) orgue et écho

These indications are almost identical; 'plan 0' looks like a misreading of 'piano'. Pierre Couprie mentioned an additional numbering on the boxes and a different order, when he visited the archives around 2005 (Couprie, 2006):

Table 4

1	251 SUR piano + echo [1,3]
2	orgue + écho [4,2]
3	Byzance: cloches + appl. Réverbérés [5,6]
4	Grelot d'Irak [7, 8]

The indications are nearly the same, except a permutation of the numbering.

The names seem to suggest what should be on the tapes:

1) A stereo piano recording

2) A stereo organ recording

3) A stereo recording of some Byzantine jewelry & percussion sounds

4) A stereo recording with some Iraqi jewelry & percussion sounds.

The examination and comparison of the tracks (Xenakis 2009) suggest that the names are not to be taken literally. First of all, every track shows echo and reverberation effects, probably combined with filtering. In detail:

1. Piano + echo: The track strangely refers to a piano sound, but does not sound like a piano. It sounds as if the tension of the strings used here is much lower than the one of a normal piano. Most authors speak about 'prepared piano' or 'probably prepared piano'.

2. Organ sounds: Since James Brody mentions the sounds of a Laotian mouth organ in 1970 (Xenakis 1970), almost every author explains these sounds as transpositions (at least one octave down) of the recording of a mouth organ from Laos. Gibson even tries to reconstruct the original recording via transposition. He writes: "*In Bohor, Xenakis improvises by playing himself the Khène [name of the Laotian mouth organ]*" (Gibson 2015 p. 89).

3. Byzance: The track is made of bell-like sounds. Some authors mention that the term 'Byzantine chant' (Harley 2009, 19) can be found in the sources, but I could not find it anywhere and no further source is given.

4. Irak: This track sounds like different kinds of small bells and small metal percussion or metal jewelry.

It is obvious that these four final stereo tapes are not recorded directly, but are the result of editing, cutting and mixing of original recordings, before echo and reverb have been added. In the archives at the Bibliothèque Nationale in Paris are at least 17 tapes that can be classified as material or production tapes for *Bohor* and five more tapes classified as different final versions of *Bohor*.

The sound 'elements' mentioned on the tape boxes are:

- 'bracelet + byzantine' [bracelet (wristband) + byzantine]
- 'cloches (?) + orgue + affolants' [bells + organ + perturbing (OR: confusion)]
- 'bracelets indonesiens' [Indonesian bracelets]
- 'cloches sans écho' [bells without echo]
- 'Affolants, bracelets (?) (Iraqi et Byzantine)' [perturbing (OR: confusion), bracelet (Iraqi and byzantine]
- 'piano' [piano]
- 'orgue et affolant' [organ and perturbing]
- 'orgue et cl.grec (?)': orgue and Greek bells
- So, the material quoted here is:
- Indonesian bracelet
- Byzantine bracelets
- Iraqi bracelet
- Organ
- Bells
- Greek bells
- Piano
- Perturbing or confusion (unclear: perhaps just mixed material?)

There is also a hand-written list of recordings for *Bohor* (Xenakis Archives OM 33-11, 9), indicating colours of blank tapes to mark single recordings (Figure 3): e.g. 'Bande II: Byzantine – entre deux roses' (tape 2: 'between two pink tapes') or 'Bande V: cloches – entre deux jaunes' (tape 5: 'between two yellow tapes'), etc.

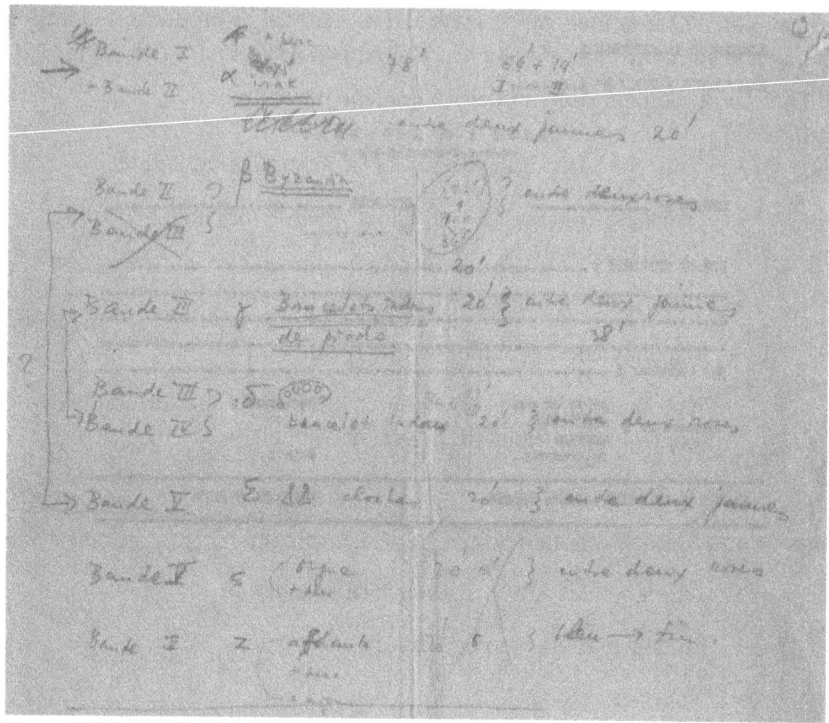

Figure 5.3: Recording list *Bohor*

Detail of OM 33-11-p09 (Archives Xenakis P), Original ca 29cm x 21 cm; List of original recordings for *Bohor*.

Listening to the mentioned tapes shows that in a first step ('original recordings') the mentioned sounds have been recorded. In the second step, some of them have been manipulated and, for example, transposed by changing the playback speed of the tape machine. Some sounds have been layered for densification, but also echo, reverberation and filtering are hearable and indicated on some tape boxes. The hearable filtering sounds like a secondary effect of reverb and echo applied. Concerning the original sounds, it can be stated that if the piano sounds were really made with a prepared piano (it is irritating that Xenakis never called them 'prepared piano'). The same holds for the organ. Xenakis never mentions a 'mouth organ' or even a 'Laotian mouth organ'. This is perplexing, as he very clearly mentions 'Iraqi bracelet', 'bracelets indonesiens' etc. There might be a simple explanation: almost from the start, the GRM-composers have been very interested in recording interesting sounds and often used the prepared piano. The piano, treated in an unusual way, played directly on the strings, etc., sounded so surprising that the audiences believed they were hearing electronic sounds. This effect was welcome as the GRM composers wanted to be honored for their electroacoustic music, not for recording instruments. So, they often kept this a secret (Friedl, 2013). Pierre Schaeffer later even claimed that it was Pierre Henry, who had invented the prepared piano simultaneously with John Cage (Schaeffer 1967, 27), which is not true (Friedl, 2013). In the middle of the 1950s, in Paris, the brothers Bernard and François Baschet started to build their own instruments and were very successful. They were explicitly inspired by Musique concrete (Frauensohn 2007, 41) and built instruments like the 'piano-tige', at times using parts of old pianos. They succeeded to migrate the piano-keyboard techniques and to apply them to completely different sound objects. In some instances, the Baschets did not only use the piano's soundboard, but also the strings and parts of the keyboard. They combined them with different resonators, including huge iron sheets. Probably their most famous instrument was the Cristal Organ ('Orgue de Cristal'). Its sounding elements are metal rods that are each connected to glass rods. If the glass rods are excited softly with wet fingers, the vibration is transmitted to the metal rods and they start to produce defined pitches, amplified with the help of a huge metal sail as a resonator. Baschet (1999) published detailed construction plans and photos of many instruments. Bernard and François Baschet founded the group *Les Structures Sonores* together with the composer Jacques Lasry and his wife, Yvonne Lasry. They started to promote the instruments and to play concerts worldwide. In 1958, when Iannis Xenakis built the Philips Pavilion at the World's Fair Exposition in Brussels, their instruments have been presented in the French Pavilion of the same exposition. In 1957 they released a first LP (Lasry Baschet, 1957) and they also performed and recorded regularly at the French Radio house, where the GRM was situated. Their music was presented in the same radio features as *musique concrète* already in the fifties (Tournet-Lammer 2006, 64). Baschet instruments have been in the studios of the French Radio ORTF from 1961 on, or earlier, as photos show (Radio France, 2018). It has to be underlined that Pierre Schaeffer's concepts around *musique concrète* was never limited to electroacoustic music, but should be applicable to all kinds of music (Schaeffer, 1966). Schaeffer invited Bernard Baschet to join the GRM that was a part of the ORTF. He became director of the research department on December 14, 1962 (Baschet F. 2007, 173) and director of the GRM from 1964 to 1966. It is beyond question that Xenakis knew the instruments of the Baschet brothers, who tried actively to convince composers to write music for their constructions. Many composers of the GRM did so, as for example Luc Ferrari (Ferrari 1963), Bernard Parmegiani (Thomas, Mion and Nattiez 1982, II), Guy Reibel (Bloch 2018), François Bayle (INA-GRM 1980, 328) or Beatriz Ferreyra (Ferreyra 1967). Listening to some recordings of the Baschet instruments (Baschet 1965) immediately evokes the sound qualities of *Bohor*.

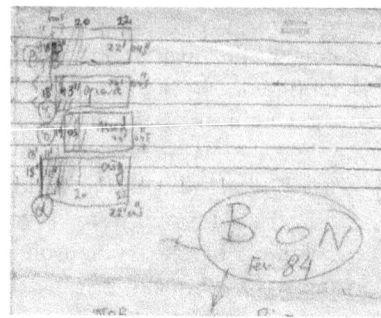

Figure 5.4: Sketch *Bohor*

Detail of OM 33-11-p15 (Archives Xenakis P), Original ca 29 cm x 21 cm, 1984.

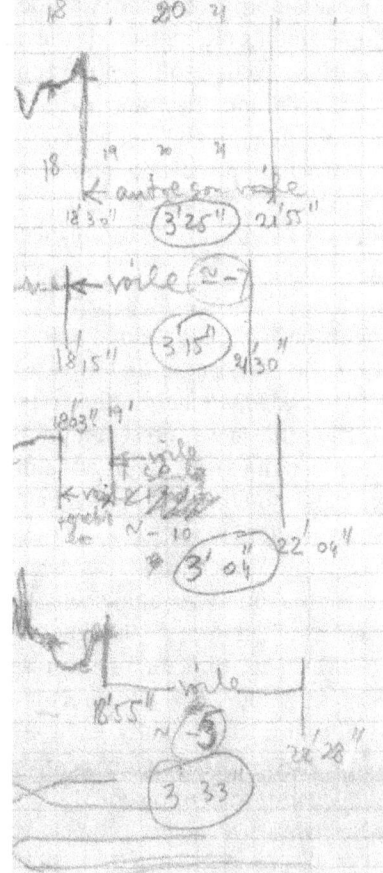

Figure 5.5: Sketch *Bohor*

Detail of OM 33-11-p8 (Archives Xenakis P), Original ca 29 cm x 21 cm, no date.

During the last three minutes of *Bohor* all tracks change, one after the other, to a broad noise, called 'white noise' in all the mentioned analyses. This 'white noise' does sound like thunder sheets. The Baschet brothers frequently integrated different kind of thunder sheets as resonators in their early instruments. In some drafts, Xenakis calls the final sounds of *Bohor* 'voile' (Xenakis Archives, OM 33-11,8) in English: 'sail' (see figure 5). The iron sheets of most of the Baschet instruments look like sails. Xenakis calls the sound in the upper system 'other sail sound' ('autre son voile'). Xenakis himself classified the three layers as high ('aigue'), medium ('medium') and low ('grave') (figure 4). He probably transposed the thunder sheet sounds. The so-called 'piano' sounds in *Bohor* do not sound like a normal piano – the high tension of the piano strings does not allow the vibrato effect that can be heard. It seems possible that Xenakis never recorded a prepared piano, but that he just used the Baschet instruments. Even the names of the tracks could refer to the Baschet instruments:

Figure 5.6: Piano-tige

Piano-tige in front of the GRM-Studio Paris, courtesy ina-GRM Paris.
piano: piano-tige or another Baschet instrument with piano
organ: cristal organ
voile: the iron sheet of Baschet instruments.

Listening to all the listed material tapes in the Xenakis Archives BnF shows, that there is no piano recorded. Instead one finds the mentioned sounds of the Baschet instruments, especially: the so-called 'prepared piano sounds' sound clearly like Baschet instruments (low tension of the piano strings, vibrato via metal sheets), as can be heard on the tapes titled 'piano' in the Xenakis Archives BnF: (*Xenakis 533 and 534*). The ending sounds called 'voile' made by metal sheets: (Xenakis 527 after 15'14" and Xenakis 529 after 15'08"). But one does not find the cristal organ, but the Laotian mouth organ sounds (Xenakis 529 after 11:40). A transposition of a part of these recordings - at least one octave down - can also be found (Xenakis 527 after 6'30"). To conclude: prepared piano and white noise have not been used in *Bohor*. It seems probable that Xenakis used instead some Baschet-Instruments or Baschet-inspired instruments at the GRM. Furthermore, he or somebody else recorded the Laotian mouth organ material.

Le Diatope / La Légende d'Eer (1978)

La Légende d'Eer is the musical part of the so-called *Diatope*, a multimedia event by Xenakis, which includes four media: text, music, light and architecture (Solomos 2003). The *Diatope* was commissioned by the Centre Beaubourg for the inauguration of the Centre George Pompidou in Paris in January 1977, the musical part by Westdeutscher Rundfunk Köln (WDR), Germany. As Xenakis had to change the proposals several times, the *Diatope* was finally premiered in Paris in July 1978. The musical part of *La Légende d'Eer* had already been premiered in the planetarium in Bochum, Germany on February 11, 1978. In both cases, the sounds were spatialised. A score, called 'partition', of the musical composition can be found in the Xenakis Archives at the BnF in Paris (Xenakis 1978 b) and a slightly different, the earlier one, in the archive of Westdeutscher Rundfunk in Cologne (Xenakis 1978 a). It might be possible that Xenakis had yet to finish this score, as Dr. Wolfgang Becker wrote him in a letter from September 1978 (Becker 1978). He mentioned that Xenakis would get the second part of his fee *"when the score is delivered"*.[5] This so-called score is pretty rudimentary and was written during the production, as sounds that have been produced in Cologne and named 'Müller' and 'James' after the assistants in the studio (Volker Müller and James Whitman) can be found in it. Volker Müller remembers that Xenakis had asked for a big drawing table to produce this score, as there was no table in the small room, where they were working in. Volker Müller unhinged a door

---

[5] „Die zweite Hälfte wird bei der Ablieferung der Partitur gezahlt werden".

and put it on an old 4-track-machine, which was not in use (Friedl 2012). Xenakis realised his score on this 'table'.

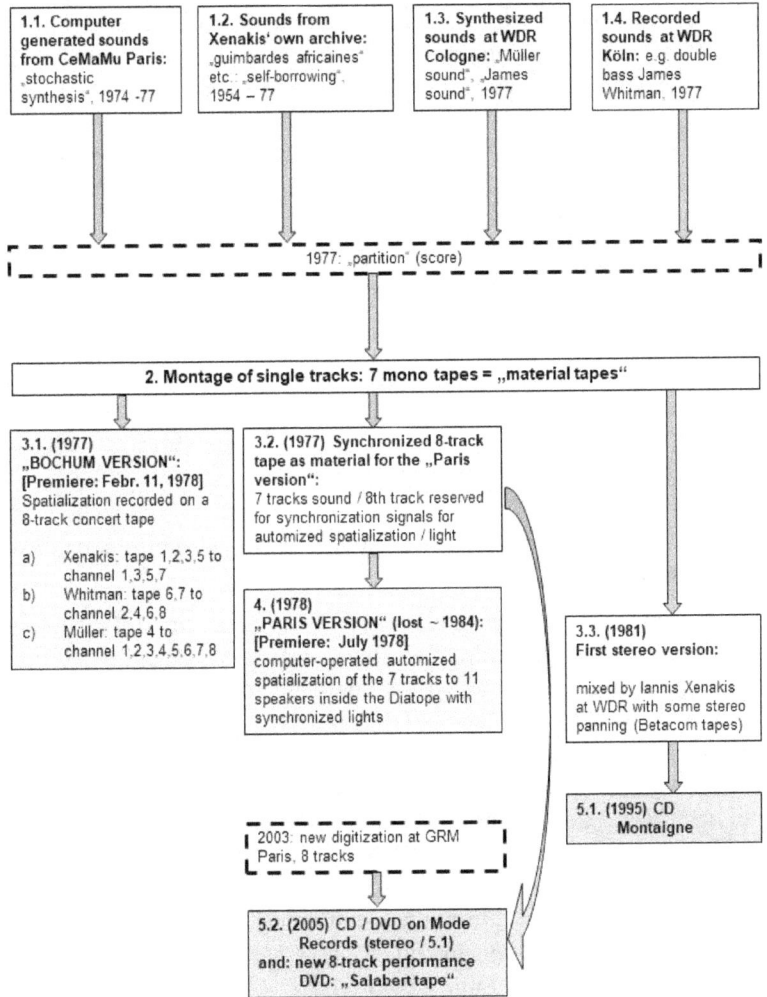

Figure 5.7: Genealogy of *La Légende d'Eer*

Production in Cologne at Elektronisches Studio des Westdeutschen Rundfunks, later mixes, digitisations and CD releases (Friedl 2015).

In 1977 Xenakis came to Cologne to produce his work at the *Studio für Elektronische Musik des WDR Köln* with some material already prepared. He brought new electronic sounds (table 1, 1.1) which he had synthesized with the help of mathematic functions in his own research center *Centre d'études de mathématique et automatique musicales (Cemamu)* in Paris (Xenakis 1974, 351 and 354) as well as sounds he had already used in other *Polytopes* (table 1, 1.2). Another sound, which became very prominent in the piece (the sound which the piece starts and ends with), was produced in Cologne together with the sound engineer of the studio, Volker Müller, on the Synthesizer EMS 100. Xenakis called this sound and its derivatives in the score *Müller* (table 1, 1.3). Furthermore, there is a recording of an extended-technique-double bass improvisation (Friedl 2012), played by James Whitman, an American composer, who assisted Xenakis for the production. Three tapes with this recording can be found in the WDR archives (Xenakis 1978 c, EL18113001, EL18113003 and EL18138002). In the montage of the 7-track mix, they can be found without any significant sound manipulation on:

track 1:   35:40 – 40:47 (length 5:07)

track 2:   35:38 – 40:17 (length: 4:49)

track 5:   24:22 – 33:27 (length 9:05).

Moreover, manipulated versions or versions with some sounds added can be found on several other tracks.

In the studio the work proceeded in several steps: first, some of the material, including the CeMaMu-sounds, the sounds produced in Cologne (but not the Müller sounds), and prerecorded sounds were manipulated (Xenakis and Kanach 2006, 355). This included filtering, reverberation, and transposition by changing the tape velocity, and various mixing techniques (table 1, 1.1 – 1.4.). These materials were used to produce the single tracks, which contain the sound materials in the final order of the piece (table 1, 2.). Seven of them had to be produced as seven different mono tracks, to be combined later in three different settings to produce the different versions of the composition. In the first setting, simple synchronisations were made (table 1, 3.2), in order to have a definite seven-track version on an eight-track tape. Xenakis took one of these tapes back to Paris and this tape was the one he was most interested in, according to Volker Müller (Friedl 2009). This was a tape without any spatialisation of the individual tracks, but almost a one-to-one synchronisation of the seven mono tapes. The reason for using only seven tracks was to reserve the eighth track for control of the spatialisation and the synchronisation with the visual part of the performance, which would happen later in the *Diatope*. This means that additional analogue control-signals were recorded on the eighth track later in Paris. The synchronisation data, the machines and the computer for realising this synchronisation and even the information of how it all worked, appears to be lost. The *Diatope* was transported to Marseille to be installed there but during the transport different parts got lost or were damaged. In 1984 the remaining parts were given away as scrap (Xenakis and Kanach 2006, 355).

Iannis Xenakis himself had mentioned three 'sound families'[6] in his text for the first commercial release of *La Légende d'Eer* on Montaigne 1995 (Xenakis 1995):

1. Instrumental music: Xenakis quotes here the 'falling Stars' (those are the sounds made by Volker Müller on the studio's synthesizer), and some other sounds he brought from Paris.

2. 'Noises' made with stones or with the help of cardboards.

3. Digital sounds made with mathematical operations in his Paris CeMaMu.

Xenakis does not mention the double bass solo by James Whitman, neither the treated double bass sounds on several tracks.

Makis Solomos provides us in his analysis with an astonishing listening protocol and a categorization of the used sounds (Solomos 2013).

He writes:

"between 27:47 and 29:01: like a slightly distorted electronic guitar in a free improvisation

from 29:28: like an improvising double bass

from 30:27: electric guitar alternating with double bass [...]"

This is the middle of the passage, where Xenakis played the uncut and untreated double bass solo by Whitman (see above: Track 5, 24:22 – 33:27 (length 9:05)). Solomos could obviously recognise the bass solo (even so he took some sul ponticello parts for electric guitar) in the mentioned CD version of Montaigne, even though it is only one track of a spatialised seven track-tape. Solomos even associated a 'free improvisation'. Marcus Erbe, who was the first to having access to the original multi track in the *Studio für*

---

[6] "Klangfamilien": astonishingly this text is printed in the booklet only in German.

elektronische Musik in Cologne, identified a 'distorted string instrument' around 38:43 (Erbe 2009).

Conclusion

The facts presented here open an interesting discussion: what is the difference between 'instrumental sounds' and a 'performance' or 'improvisation'? This discussion is not trivial, not least as it has a serious legal impact: an improviser or performer could have asked for copyrights, somebody who just records some sounds, cannot. The question behind the legal aspect is the nature of electroacoustic music: can a 10-minute solo improvisation be used uncut in a way that it becomes proprietary material of the composer? Today, after all the experiences with sampling, we would probably say 'no'. But we were no witnesses of the recordings and nobody knows if, and if 'yes', which instructions Xenakis gave the players.

Why did Xenakis not mention the performers? Xenakis did not mention who recorded the Laotian Mouth organ (or if it was himself), neither he mentioned Volker Müller, who performed the synthesizer-sounds in *La Legende d'Eer* that are used without alterings (and even called 'Müller' in the score and classified as 'instrumental sounds' by Xenakis himself (Xenakis 1995)), and he did not mention James Whitman as the creator of the original bass solo. He mentioned their names in the 'score' (Müller and James), but nobody knew who they were; Solomos guessed that 'Müller' describes the 'randomized oscillations' as the German word 'Müller' means 'miller' (Solomos 2003, 7). The 'score' was never published. Finally, the 'score' is no score. The double bass passages are missing, and a lot of other sounds are also not indicated. This 'score' was probably an aide memoire for the mix and then was delivered as 'partition' to Dr. Becker, in order to get the second rate of the commission fee paid (Becker 1978).

One more open question is: if Xenakis himself did not think about this sound material as 'performed music', in this case, it would be astonishing that he used it without any further treatment or manipulation. The label 'instrumental sound' seems to point in this direction, but is a ten-minute-long improvisation (if it was an improvisation and not a verbal score) still a 'sound'?

Another possible explanation for this practice is that Xenakis did not want others to know the original sources. On the one hand, he was a specialist of mathematical structures and concentrated his writing and interviews around this topic, on the other hand, it was a common behavior among electroacoustic musicians not to tell others how their sounds were made. For example, one of the closest friends of Xenakis at that time, Luc Ferrari, seemed to have remained silent about his extensive use of inside-piano sounds, and most listeners with untrained ears would still think today, that those sounds have been produced electronically (Friedl 2013). The same holds true for the sounds used in *Bohor*, no analysis realises that the 'white noise' is, in fact, the (treated) sound of metal sails or Baschet instruments, and the same also holds true for the so-called 'prepared piano' sounds.

Xenakis was a flexible composer and obviously responsive to musical inspirations around him. Even though he focused on his mathematical aims, he did not hesitate to use whatever convinced him practically. It remains unclear why he did not credit the human performers of sound material in his electroacoustic compositions: did he think about the recordings as neutral sound material, or did he try to hide some wonderful human sound sources?

Bibliography

Baschet, François. 1999. *Les scuptures sonores – The Sound Sculptures of Bernard and François Baschet*. Chelmsford: Soundworld.

Baschet, François. 2007. *Mémoires sonores*. Paris: L'Harmattan.

Bloch, Thomas. 2018. Personal website, http://www.thomasbloch.net/f_cristal-baschet.html (Accessed 18 April 2018).

Becker, Wolfgang. 1978. *Letter to Iannis Xenakis from September 27, 1978*. Köln: Archiv Westdeutscher Rundfunk, Historisches Archiv 05623, unpublished.

Chion, Michel. 1972. "Vingt années de musique électroacoustique." In *Musique en Jeu 8*. Paris: Seuil.

Couprie, Pierre. 2006. "Une analyse détaillée de Bohor". In *Definitive Proceedings of the International Symposium Iannis Xenakis (Athens May 2005)*, edited by Makis Solomos, http://www.iannis-xenakis.org/Articles/Couprie.pdf. (Accessed 18 April 2018).

Erbe, Marcus. 2009. Klänge schreiben: Die Transkriptionsproblematik elektroakustischer Musik. Wien: Verlag Der Apfel.

Ferrari, Luc.1963. Bachiques [score]. IRCAM 2018. http://brahms.ircam.fr/works/work/36392/ (Accessed 18 April 2018).

Fleuret, Maurice.1962."Vingt-cinq ans après sa mort. Faut-il prendre congé de Ravel?" *France Observateur*. 27 December, 1962, 17-18, cited from: Benoît Gibson. 2015. "À propos de Bohor (1962) de Iannis Xenakis." In *Iannis Xenakis, La Musique électroacoustique, Proceedings of the International Symposium (23-25 May 2012)*, edited by Makis Solomos. Paris: L'Harmattan, 84.

Frauensohn, Danièle. 2007. *Bernard Baschet, Chercheur et sculpteur de sons*. Paris: L'Harmattan.

Friedl, Reinhold. 2009. "Polyphone Monophonie" In Musiktexte 122. Köln, 12-17.

Friedl, Reinhold. 2012. "Was ist ein Fehler? – Xenakis' La Légende d'Eer: Versuch einer kritischen Edition elektroakustischer Musik" Musiktexte 135, 33-39.

Friedl, Reinhold. 2013. Das Klavier in der elektroakustischen Musik [radio feature]. Köln: Westdeutscher Rundfunk, Archivnummer 5187 849. Broadcast: 16 October 2013.

Friedl, Reinhold 2015. "Towards a Critical Edition of Electroacoustic Music: Xenakis – La Légende d'Eer." In *Iannis Xenakis, La musique électroacosutique*, edited by Makis Solomos. Paris: L'Harmattan, 109-122.

Gayou, Évelyne 2007. *Le GRM, Groupe de Recherches Musicales: Cinquante ans d'histoire, Les chemins de la musique*. Paris: Fayard.

Gibson, Benoît 2015. "À propos de Bohor (1962) de Iannis Xenakis." In *Iannis Xenakis, La Musique électroacoustique, Proceedings of the International Symposium (23-25 May 2012)*, edited by Makis Solomos. Paris: L'Harmattan, 83-96.

Harley, James. 2002. "The electroacoustic Music of Iannis Xenakis". *Computer Music Journal*, 26. Cambridge: MIT Press.

Harley, James 2004. *Xenakis: His life in music*. New York: Routledge.

Harley, James 2009. "Continuities and Changes in the Electroacoustic Music by Iannis Xenakis." In *Iannis Xenakis: Das elektroakustische Werk*, edited by Ralph Paland and Christoph von Blumröder.Wien: Verlag Der Apfel, 17-27.

Hünermann, Tobias. 2009. "Iannis Xenakis: Bohor." In *Iannis Xenakis: Das elektroakustische Werk*. Wien: Verlag der Apfel, 152-166.

INA-GRM (ed.). 1980. *Répertoire Acousmatique 1948-1980*. Paris: Institut National de l'Audiovisuel.

INA-GRM a, *Registre des Originaux*, [pdf]; by courtesy of Geneviève Bayle-Mâche.

INA-GRM b, [Excel file], List of tape archive GRM; by courtesy of Daniel Teruggi and Yann Geslin.

Kim, Rebecca 2004. *Iannis Xenakis's Bohor* (1962). www.music.columbia.edu/masterpieces/notes/xenakis/index.html. (Accessed 17 April 2018), www.music.columbia.edu/~liubo/bohor/present/ (Accessed 16 April 2016).

Radio France. 2017. *Bernard Baschet au temps du Traité des Objets Musicaux (1964-1966)*. https://www.franceculture.fr/emissions/creation-air/bernard-baschet-au-temps-du-traite-des-objets-musicaux-1964-1966. (Accessed 17 April 2018).

Schaeffer, Pierre. 1966. *Traité des objets musicaux*. Paris: Editions du Seuil.

Schaeffer, Pierre. 1967. *La musique concrète*. Paris: Presses universitaires de France.

Solomos, Makis. 2003. *Le Diatope et La Légende d'Eer*, www.iannis-xenakis.org/fxe/actus/Solom3.pdf (Accessed April 18 2018).

Thomas, Jean-Christophe, Mion, Philippe, and Nattiez, Jean-Jacques. 1982. *L'envers d'une œuvre, De Natura Sonorum de Bernard Parmegiani*. Paris: Èditions Buchet/Chastel, Institut de l'Audiovisuel.

Tournet-Lammer, Jocelyne. 2006. *Sur les traces de Pierre Schaeffer*. Paris: Institut National de l'Audiovisuel.

Turner, Charales. 2015. "Why Bohor?" *Iannis Xenakis, La Musique électroacoustique, Proceedings of the International Symposium, 23-25 (May 2012)*, edited by Makis Solomos. Paris: L'Harmattan, 99-108.

Xenakis, Iannis. 1974. "Les polytopes de Beaubourg." In *Musique de l'architecture*, 2006, edited by Iannis Xenakis and Sharon Kanach. Marseille: Editions Paranthèses, 347-351.

Xenakis, Iannis. 1978 a. *La Légende d'Eer (Musique du Diatope) - Partition resumée definitive des 7 pistes sonores* [score]. Köln: Archiv Westdeutscher Rundfunk, Orch.Part. 16405, unpublished.

Xenakis, Iannis. 1978 b. *La Légende d'Eer - Partition* [score]. In Makis Solomos. 2003. *Le Diatope et La Légende d'Eer*, 33-36, www.iannis-xenakis.org/fxe/actus/Solom3.pdf. (Accessed 18 April 2018).

Xenakis, Iannis. 2006. *Musique de l'architecture*. Edited by Sharon Kanach. Marseille: Editions Paranthèses.

Audio Sources

Baschet, Bernard and Baschet, François. 1965. *Structures For Sound* [LP]. Paris: BAM – LD 087.

Baschet, Lasry. 1957. *Les Nouvelles Structures Sonores* [LP]. Paris: Ducretet Thompson. https://www.discogs.com/de/Lasry-Baschet-Les-Nouvelles-Structures-Sonores/release/11468910 (Accessed 17 April 2018).

Ferreyra, Beatriz. 1967. *Demeures aquatiques* [magnetic tape]. In Ferreyra, B. 2015. GRM Works [LP], Wien: Mego REGRM 015.

Xenakis, Iannis. 1970. The Electro-acoustic Music [LP], New York: Nonesuch H-71246.

Xenakis, Iannis. 1978 c. *La Légende d'Eer Material Tapes* [Magnetic tape]. Köln: Westdeutscher Rundfunk, Tonbandarchiv, unpublished.

Xenakis, Iannis. 1995. *La Légende d'Eer* [CD]. Paris: Auvidis Montaigne MO 782058, Paris: re-released with different cover (2002). Paris: AuvidisMontaigne, MO 782144.

Xenakis, Iannis. 2009. *Bohor* [data DVD 8 tracks for concert performance]. Paris: Durand-Salabert-Eschig. Xenakis-Archives P, private archive of the Xenakis family, Paris.

Xenakis 527 – Xenakis 543, [magnetic tape]. Archives Xenakis BnF. Paris: Bibliothèque National de France, unpublished.

Chapter 6

Performing *Nomos alpha* by Iannis Xenakis: reflections on interpretative space

Alfia Nakipbekova

Introduction: the Xenakian cello

> *"Composers like Xenakis challenge us to reevaluate from scratch our most basic assumptions about music – a very good thing for us to do periodically. Every generation produces a few artists who force us to return to the beginning, to strip away all existing notions of art and reconceptualize it from the ground up."*
> (Thomas DeLio 2001, 241)

Nomos alpha by Iannis Xenakis is one of the most significant late twentieth-century compositions that embody this predication. For the performer, the discovery and the process of mastering the work marks the beginning of a re-evaluation not only of the particular cello techniques involved in the piece, but, in many ways, the fundamental questions of interpretation and performance. Xenakis had a fresh perspective on the instruments – their sonorities and potential for colours and textures. With *Nomos alpha* he 'invented' a 'new' instrument, 'reconceptualised from the ground up', which, however, contains the 'memory' of the traditional cello in its physical shape and attributes with traces of identifiable cello sound and the player's gestures. Except for the innovative *scordatura* method, Xenakis employs the cello in a conventional manner, i.e. eschewing non-instrumental means for sound production employed by some of the composers of his time. He creates the sonorities and percussive timbre, for example, by the *battuto* bowing, *sul ponticello* and *pizzicati*, extending and combining these techniques in a distinctly new way. The cellist is required to step beyond the learned instrumental habits and techniques, venturing on a journey of developing her/his personal perspective on the singular playing mode. Yet, the conventional technical methods are part of the Xenakian cello's history, as they continue being rediscovered and renewed. It is my belief that the process of mastering the radical system of physical responses in *Nomos alpha* must be supported by the instrumental foundation that has been ingrained, at the earlier stages of instrumental learning, in the cellist's subconscious mind and muscle memory. Developing Xenakian cello methods refine the visceral connection to the instrument by experimenting and expanding the traditional technical and practice procedures. Xenakis's writing challenges the cellist to develop the 'extended' practice that encompasses the elements of pure physicality, intellect and imagination, towards the level where they converge into an integrated domain of the *philosophy of cello technique*. At the beginning of the journey, an intellectual grasp of the score requires much research and study. Later, the uncommon physical intensity involved in practising and performing *Nomos alpha* becomes the most pressing issue to resolve. In the course of five years of my close study and practice, a number of live performances (in different venues, experimenting with various formats) and recording, two elements have chrystallised: 1. The importance of continuous training rooted in the established norms of playing that is also directed towards advancing the technique further, far beyond these norms.[1] 2. The increasing role of the intuitive and interdisciplinary paths in investigating *Nomos alpha*'s interpretative space. This chapter focuses on the two domains within the broad areas above: a singular philosophy of interpretation and technique embodied in *Nomos alpha*, and the Associative Method – an extended approach for internalising the composition. In this regard, I will discuss some of the distinctive imagery and artistic concepts of the cinematographer Andrei Tarkovsky evinced in his film *Stalker* (1979), and their relevance to the development of *Nomos alpha*'s interpretative space in my extended practice.

Interpretative space

My approach to interpretation consists of three aspects: structural, performative (including the aspects of physicality and theatricality) and technical (in which 'technique' is a part of a broader term of 'instrumentalism'). These aspects are mutually inclusive: interpretative space encompasses the notions of both technique and interpretation. *Techniques* are expressive tools, the means for shaping sounds and musical gestures. William Pleeth (1992, 2), known for his integral pedagogical approach, notes:

---

[1] This relates to every aspect of cello technique: sound production, left- and right-hands techniques. It is a two-way process that nourishes both modes of playing, connecting the traditional and 'extreme' technical styles. Xenakis's music influenced my approach to the traditional concert repertoire, in many ways modifying my perceptions of the possibilities of sound, articulation and tone.

> *"'Technique', in its fullest sense, means discovering and developing the physical means for bringing into existence a piece of music. Thus it follows that technique per se cannot exist apart from the music it is meant to serve."*

John Rink (2003, 321) affirms the technical dimension as an intrinsic part of artistry:

> *"Artistry involves the ability to make performance more than the sum of its parts, including the influences of history, analysis and much else (not least the technical dimension, so often ignored in the literature on performance). Artistry involves close and peripheral vision all at once, especially in the moment of truth."*

In *Nomos alpha* Xenakis expands the cello's domain of expression to a new level transcending instrumental possibilities (for his time, and in some sense, for the present), propounding the questions of performability, interpretation and the status of the performer. Thinking in terms of *interpretative space* rather than *interpretation* opens up the possibilities of expression where the division between 'technique' and 'interpretation' is no longer relevant. Nouritza Matossian (2005, 238) asserts the pertinence of the techniques to the expression of compositional ideas in the piece:

> *"Since there can be no elaboration of thematic, melodic or harmonic development, colour and texture occupy the stage. Particular modes of playing such as pizzicato, col legno, battuto, sul ponticello with tremolo [...] take on a primary function – not textural filling but as geological features forming the crust of this landscape."* [2]

Nomos alpha is among Xenakis's compositions that have attracted extensive mathematical, compositional and structural analysis. Among these studies, the composer's detailed explanation provides the theoretical basis for apprehending his compositional concepts (Xenakis 1992); in addition, the writings by Fernand Vandenbogaerde (1968), Thomas DeLio (1980), Jan Vriend (1981), Matoussian (2005), Makis Solomos (1993; 1997), Robert Peck (2003), Moreno Andreatta and Carlos Agon (2007), and Christian Utz (2016), among others, encompass the broad range of the work's problematics: from the

---

[2] One of the prominent Xenakis's performers, cellist Peter Strauch (2011, 14) suggests: *"You have to take each sound as it is, not as colouring, but as a distinct object."*

mathematical procedures to the performer's interpretative choices. For example, Peck elucidates these choices by highlighting the structural layers of the compositions and their relationship within the two Paths,[3] suggesting various strategies for the performer.

Although intellectual understanding of the composition, as an ongoing investigation of its abstract concepts, together with performance theory, is an important aspect in shaping interpretation, the new physical and mental challenges posed by Xenakis – such as an extremely high degree of control and stamina – can only be met through the total effort, involving intense physicality and the deepest layers of the performer's personal power of *intent*. The interpretative space that progressively evolves and then takes shape during a live performance is the result of this totality, in which instrumental 'athleticism' combined with an acute awareness and attention to the smallest adjustments of the muscles involved, constitutes a significant aspect. The notion of intent, repeatedly evoked by Xenakis, contains a potential to transcend the material effort of playing, and is an integral part of the endeavour. As noted by some of Xenakis's performers, a prolonged and profoundly committed striving to master his works may result in the 'alchemic' transformation of an extreme physical and mental tension into a transcendental state or 'trance' experiences. A percussionist Ying-Hsueh Chen (2017) comments on her experience of this dimension in performing Xenakis's music:

> "I was intrigued a couple times by 'trance experience' when I play multi percussion pieces, especially by Iannis Xenakis. I feel literally that I was led to using the reptile brain to perform Xenakis, and if my mind interferes in one second, I will fail. By surprise, audiences would come to me and express that they were in a deep mental and spiritual state while listening to me playing Xenakis."

Another prominent performer of Xenakis's music Franck Reinecke (2006) conveys his deeply felt responses in his performances of *Theraps*:

> "This music has catapulted me out into space...into the ocean. On the other hand, it has given me freedom – a freedom, however, which doesn't let me do whatever I want, but a freedom which leaves me it up to me how to survive this whole thing. That's freedom under pressure. It's a great tension."

---

[3] Path 1 and Path 2 are the two contrasting structural layers of *Nomos alpha* that comprise the twenty-four sections. DeLio (1980, 63) uses the terms Level 1 and Level 2.

Experimenting with various formats – performing on acoustic cello (with pre-record), electric cello and two acoustic cellos – expanded my interpretative resources. The idea of using the electric cello was initially dictated by the practicality of retuning during performance as well as transportation considerations.[4] Later, the differences between the nature of the sound and physicality of playing on the electric cello offered additional interpretative variants. Electric cello's shorter fingerboard alters the perceptions of spatiality – the techniques feel more condensed, the glissandi trajectories are 'geographically' shortened, the tempi feel more compressed – as if the sense of temporality is affected by this new spatial awareness. In a standing position, the balance between the legs and the arms has to be readjusted and the range of the movements expanded, so the choreography of playing becomes a part of the interpretative space. The 'dancing' cellist occupies the visual dimension of the performance that merges with the sound and the temporal processes. Although, in some ways, the posture is freer and more dynamic, the cellist has to incorporate some subtle realignments of the body in relation to the instrument during performance to counteract destabilisation of the left hand's manoeuvres around the electric cello's virtual body. Additionally, in contrast to the acoustic cello's smoothness of the fingerboard, the fret markings (raised dots indicating positions) on the electric cello add a particular tactility of a striated surface, disrupting the sliding and oscillating motion in glissandi and microtones. This element of material 'resistance', paradoxically, provokes instinctive softening of the left hand – the awareness of the fret markings imbues the movements with increased plasticity. Performing with two acoustic cellos introduces a strong element of theatricality – the repeated action of exchanging the cellos marks clearly the boundaries between the two Paths (sections two, three, five and

---

[4] Xenakis's scordatura in *Nomos alpha* presents a unique practical problem: the (gut) C string must be detuned down one octave in three instances and a major second in one (bar 295) and retuned three times; in addition, in the second section of the Path Two (bar 117) detuning must be executed *while* playing. The action of retuning is more challenging as the rapidly increasing pressure disturbs the acoustic cello's body, particularly, in the case of an older, more sensitive instrument. Experimenting with using a robust, cruder factory cello in one of my performances, confirmed my belief in the importance of the *tone* quality in *Nomos alpha* – although it is not meant to be 'beautiful' in a conventional sense, it has to resonate with clarity and variety of timbres. Unpredictability in the action of the cello pegs is another problematic aspect; replacing the traditional peg set with a new type, which provides a reliable, smooth response, does not completely resolve this issue. Performing on the electric cello (with ratchet tuning pegs) eliminates this obstacle, at the same time demanding a number of other technical and practical adjustments.

six). The choreography of these exchanges become a part of the performance and have to be either staged or executed with the intuitive spontaneity of the moment – as a gestural comment on the interactions between the temporal dimensions and textures of the two Paths. The two cellos, then, are involved in a dialogue, each 'character' presenting their 'case' – it is neither a confrontation nor an agreement. The final part of the 'play' however, requires an additional performer (unless performed with a pre-recorded part) to realise the procession of the two-tiered scalic strands, crossing over and then moving in the opposite directions, receding inexorably into the Infinity.

Continuity and the extended techniques

The range of the extended techniques employed by Xenakis in *Nomos alpha* contains left- and right- hands techniques that have already been used widely in the first half of the twentieth century (except a particular use of quartertones in the context of other textures, and scordatura, as noted above). Most of these techniques are familiar to cellists and are not excessively challenging, although each type of method is further extended and refined (for example, Xenakian sul ponticello is a 'Pandora's box' that contains the full spectrum of 'treasures' – sounds, noise and textures – from coruscating sonorities to grinding blocks of sound). What is new and unusually difficult is the manner in which they are combined in the dense score and the ferocity of the rapid changes of pitches, textures, dynamics and the assemblages of the smaller and larger units. This complex body of information must be processed and translated into the physical movements simultaneously, at an expeditious pace.[5] In the following section, I will discuss the two areas within these techniques – glissandi and extreme dynamics – the notable characteristics of *Nomos alpha*, which express the interaction between the fabric of the sound and the work's temporal pulsation.

Nomos alpha presents a challenge of developing meta-fast responses for sustaining continuity within discontinuity – the pauses (abrupt stoppages) and sharply defined series of techniques (actions). The notion of *continuity* is central to Xenakis's approach in his architectural and musical works. In *Synaphaï* (1969), for example, the continuity must be achieved by a 'liquid articulation' – a

---

[5] Similarly, with regards to the extreme technical difficulties presented by his scores, Brian Ferneyhough (1995, 372) notes that these techniques are generally familiar to the performers from their experiences in other contexts, however, *"what is unfamiliar is, firstly, the unusual rapidity with which these elements unfold and succeed one another, secondly, the high level of informational density in notational terms, and, thirdly, the extreme demands made on the performer's technique and powers of concentration."*

proposal that implies the composer's interest in writing music that goes against the piano's nature (Terrazas 2010, 44). In his conversation with Bálint András Varga (1996, 90) Xenakis elaborates on this idea: 'the basic question of *Evryali* was to achieve continuity on the instrument which has an opposite nature.' This suggests that Xenakis's motivation for writing instrumental music was in part, to search for the sounds produced by the instruments outside their broadly perceived boundaries. In *Nomos alpha* the composer explores the 'opposite nature' of the cello – percussiveness, extremes of registers and 'unnaturally' rapid, wide leaps across the fingerboard, with wildly fluctuating dynamics; at the same time, the continuity of sound is expressed through the abundant sonorities of glissandi. Playing glissandi in this context creates a new sensation in the relationship with the instrument – a particular physicality of connecting the left hand with the fingerboard in the repeated vertical movements of various lengths in combination with other techniques. The composition contains a rich assemblage of glissandi that have distinct qualities and characteristics of multiple acclivities and speeds. In the tightly structured sound-environment of *Nomos alpha*, the 359 glissandi are audial expressions of continuity and transformation – as the single entities or 'distinct objects' that are coalesced into clusters and textures. Another function of this compositional tool is highlighting and sustaining the overall ambiguous pitch environment; the relationship between glissandi, microtones and quartertones is a significant aspect and one of the extreme technical challenges of the piece. The fluctuating dynamics function as an expression of spatiality, creating an audial impression of moving 'particles' charged with various speeds. The spatial dimension is generated by oscillations between various degrees of *piano* and *forte* –the lowest dynamic marking being *pppp* (the Path Two, bb. 46, 64 and 111), and the highest *fff* dispersed densely throughout the score. This effect is particularly vivid in the recorded versions of *Nomos alpha* – recording techniques offer possibilities for manipulating the sound to some extent (although this factor does not play a substantial role in the overall interpretative concept). Live performance, however, contains the additional visual and theatrical dimensions communicated through the physicality of the performance process and a strong sense of the performer's intent.

Xenakis is known for his belief in the universal interconnectedness in life and the arts, asserting that 'all paintings, music, all the works of every age meet at some point' (Bois 1996, 21). Xenakis's brief reference to the paintings of Mondrian, Malevich and Klee in his conversation with Mario Bois has drawn my attention to the images of the *grid* and the macro/micro dimensions in Xenakis's music generally and specifically in *Nomos alpha*, and the possibility of approaching some of the instrumental challenges from this perspective.[6] Matossian (2005, 238) depicts the composition's developmental processes as juxtaposition of macro and micro dimensions:

> *"Micro-events follow macrostructures in close juxtaposition to reveal similarities of structure at different levels; a micro-photograph next to an aerial shot or a zoom followed by a wide pan is an identifiable movement of Nomos alpha."*

She asserts the uniqueness of the structure that exhibits 'a sharp polarity in the scale of magnitude, between the very small and very large' and eloquently describes the cosmological allusions in Xenakis's music:

> *"The imagery which nourishes his music has removed the anthropocentric vision of the universe, replacing it with the poetics of the galaxies and nebulae millions of light years away, the wars of electrons and atoms splitting with deadly force, and the never-ending journeys of wayward gas molecules."* (Matossian 1986, 244)

The poetic imagery stimulates the performer's imagination as a tool for finding alternative solutions outside the conventional methods of practising, i.e. combining necessary physical repetitions with mental 'mapping' – changing perspectives by 'zooming in' on the events, and then expanding the focus on its larger sections – grouping the events into the units that are held together by a centre of 'gravity' and finding a physical approach required to integrate these elements into a single gesture (see Examples 6. 1 and 6. 2).

Example 6.1: *Nomos alpha*, **bars 219-222**

© Copyright 1967 by Boosey & Hawkes Music Publishers Ltd. Reproduced by permission of Boosey & Hawkes Music Publishers Ltd.

---

[6] Xenakis recalls: *"I came across the painting of Mondrian quite by chance […] We were trying to find a way of illustrating our calculations: it was thus that we noticed the role played by the grid in regard to Klee's and Mondrian's concept of painting, and similarly in all kinds of sciences and human expressions."* (Bois 1980, 21)

Performing Nomos alpha by Iannis Xenakis

One can think of the first bar in this grouping (bar 219) consisting of five light, 'shimmering' glissandi sliding rapidly upwards across the strings and the fingerboard, as a transitional gesture, focusing on the next event beginning with the heavy accent that gives a momentum to the double-line crossing glissando passage. The three bars in this excerpt may be viewed as the two distinct elements consisting of one (bar 219) and two bars (bars 220-221) that occur on two spatial planes – the first one at some distance, the second at the close range.

Example 6.2: *Nomos alpha,* **bars 269-273**

©Copyright 1967 by Boosey & Hawkes Music Publishers Ltd. Reproduced by permission of Boosey & Hawkes Music Publishers Ltd.

Here (Example 6. 2) the central accent of the grouping falls in the middle of the glissando in double stops across the A and D strings *fff* (bar 273), following the three bars of the 'throbbing' double stop where the focus is on the bow – a moment of stability which provides a brief rest for the left hand.

The rapid fluctuations of the sound registers, duration and speed expressed through combinatorial use of the dynamics and glissandi, create a particular pulse throughout the composition, a 'perpetual pulsation', as described by Varga in his conversation with Xenakis (Varga 1996, 64), in the composer words: 'with the dynamics and accents, there come different multiple rhythms as well' (Ibid.) In my practice, the imagery of the 'map' of this pulsation contained within the metrical grid of *Nomos alpha,* gives an interpretive key to the complexity of the composition. With practice and many performances, the piece's contours come to life as a part of a global sonic organism – in the overarching view of the structure, the beginning and the end meet as if completing the circle of transformations: the first note C (in the middle register, pizzicato, *fff*, in the state of high density) dissolves into the final C (in the lowest register, arco, con sordino, *ppp*, in the opposite state of sparsity). (See Examples 6. 3 and 6. 4).

On a purely physical plane, grouping the 'distinct objects' into clusters across the quadruple metric grid provides momentary pauses generating patterns of instinctive tension and release.

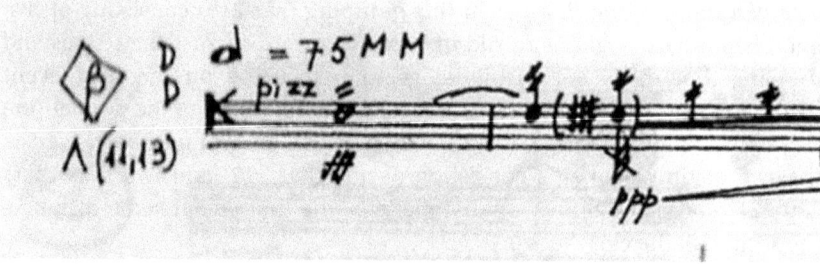

Example 6.3: Bars 1-2

© Copyright 1967 by Boosey & Hawkes Music Publishers Ltd. Reproduced by permission of Boosey & Hawkes Music Publishers Ltd.

Example 6.4: Bars 382-383

© Copyright 1967 by Boosey & Hawkes Music Publishers Ltd. Reproduced by permission of Boosey & Hawkes Music Publishers Ltd.

Performing silences

"Sound should evoke silence and not abolish it."
(Sylvio Gualda 2010, 164)

The composition's singular instrumental complexities include the capacity to sustain the continuity of events within discontinuity of the textures – the isochronal and irregular stops, breaks between the Paths and disruptions incurred by detuning manipulations. The interpretation of *Nomos alpha* encompasses both the musical gestures and the silences: the ruptures occurring *within* the events, *between* the events and at the intersection that (dis)connects the two Paths. The multiplicity of their characteristics and functions are expressed by: 1. notated rests (143 in total) as a part of the texture; 2. transitions between the sections; 3. pauses as a technical necessity (i.e., for detuning). Focusing on *transitions* and *in-betweenness* provokes redistribution of energies within the structural grid, integrating the glissandi into the structure with multiple 'perforations' of silences: the pauses inscribed between the events and the larger blocks of sound, commas in the section five of the Path Two, caesura between the two Paths, fermatas, accidental ruptures and detuning stoppages. These moments are expressed either by a 'clean' abrupt stop or by a gradual transition – the sound morphing into silence. The pulsation of the performance process occurs on multiple levels: the sound, the structure/texture correlations, the fluctuations and inconsistencies, disruptions, and relentlessness of a musician performing in living time. The silences (pauses) are part of this process, each moment containing its own duration and depth – these junctures are marked by intensities created by the performer's physical movements. Performing silences is physically and emotionally demanding; interpretation of the pauses is an artistic choice, often made by spontaneous decisions based on the intuitive grasp of the structure and physicality of the moment. The silences offer the possibilities for improvisation within the structure. According to Ferneyhough (1995, 402), the score itself is 'not a plan for an "ideal" performance'. For Ferneyhough, the 'notation-realisation relationship' of his scores offers possibilities and 'space to move' for the performer; the network of silences occupies the 'underground' as rhizomatic proliferation within the sound.

> "For me, silence – by which I mean also 'functional silence' [...] is far from being a neutral medium for spacing out events: I see it [...] as a disembodied 'ether' capable of acting as an energized vehicle for the 'silent continuation' of fragmented developmental structures." (Ferneyhough 1995, 382)

This concept is summarised:

> "JB: in other words, silence may simply represent phases during which particular processes are 'hidden' from view, much as a stream may disappear beneath the ground, only to re-appear at another point; they don't necessarily signify a suspension of action or arrested motion." (Ibid.)

Awareness of these 'hidden processes' – the moments of silences between the sounds and the events subtly shapes and reshapes the dynamics of the choreographic expression. 'Performing silences' is also a structural tool, which can be employed to illuminate the contours of the composition's global configuration, 'setting' its larger and smaller components (sections, sub-sections and events of the Path One) into its temporal frame. Xenakis (Varga 1996, 63) articulates his viewpoint on this subject:

> "Silence is always a surprise. [...] During silence we can think over what we have heard and understand it better [...] Silence is difficult. We can regard it as the suspension of action, but also as a state before explosion. Its timing therefore is not simple."

The two Paths are clearly differed in their consistencies of the sonorities – the silences notated as commas between the single pitches suspended in the high register, are the exceptions in the ubiquitous perpetuity of the sound in the Path Two. (See Example 6. 5)

Example 6.5: Bars 234-239

© Copyright 1967 by Boosey & Hawkes Music Publishers Ltd. Reproduced by permission of Boosey & Hawkes Music Publishers Ltd.

Xenakis continues:

> "And another thing: music is sound, that is action. If there's no music, there is silence. In other words, silence is the negation of music." (Varga 1996, 63)

However, in *Nomos alpha* pauses (silences) are the integral component of the structure that functions to delineate the events in the kaleidoscopic interplay of the rhythmical patterns. Performing silences constitutes both *action* and *state* as a subliminal condition of awareness of the transformational processes that occur on various levels. In live realisation of *Nomos alpha*, the performer lives each moment of silence through her/his body. A particular physicality involved in performing Xenakis's instrumental music generates a distinctly Xenakian 'carnal knowledge' and is, in itself, 'interpretation'.[7]

---

[7] The notion of 'carnal relationship' with the musical composition is investigated by Elizabeth Le Guin (2006, 14). She states: "*Because the performer's relationship to the work of art must have an extensively explored bodily element, a performing identification with a composer is based on a particular type of knowledge which could be called carnal.*"

Associative Method

"Myself, I wanted to deal with the abysses that surround us and among which we live. The most formidable are those of our destiny, of life or of death, visible and invisible universes. [...]. Rational knowledge coalesces with intuitive knowledge, or revelation. It is impossible to dissociate one from the other." (Xenakis 1987, 32)

Xenakis values intuition and imagination in the creative process – his idea of 'a thousand different ways' of interpretation is an important statement for the performer to consider:

"Every musical piece is like a complex rock, formed by ridges and designs engraved within and without, that can be interpreted in a thousand different ways without a single one being the best or the most true. By virtue of this multiple exegesis, music inspires all sorts of fantastic imaginings, like a Crystal catalyst." (Xenakis 1987, 32)

Xenakis's musical ideas were nourished by his vigorous interests in diverse subjects such as Ancient Greek theatre, mathematics, philosophy and electronic sound. In the above quotation, his reference to 'all sorts of fantastic imaginings' may suggest a possibility of an indirect approach to the interpretative space, involving subjective associations from the performer's own culture, experiences, and various disciplines and art genres. Exploration of associations with the art forms that resonate with the interpreter's artistic disposition (cinematography, literature and theatre, for example) offers a distinct perspective in extended practice, as a way of discerning and connecting to the heart of the work of art through the prism of another. I term this pathway for approaching the interpretative space as the Associative Method, an unstructured process of following freely the intuitive connections between the musical work and other forms of expression, perceived through synchronicities, images, memories and spontaneous 'revelations'. My subjective response grew from the effort involved in the study of Xenakis's music – a process, which, 'like a Crystal catalyst', intensified the experience of subliminal affinity with other forms of artistic investigation.

Exploration *Nomos alpha*'s spatial and temporal processes reactivated my interest in Andrei Tarkovsky's singular cinematic interpretation of Arcady and Boris Strugatsky's novella *Roadside Picnic* (1972) in his film *Stalker* (1979). Tarkovsky's films contain a rich spectrum of themes and imagery; in *Stalker* the concepts of Time and Temporality are embodied in the recurring visual images of the tunnels and water. In the canon of his seven films, the textures of the four elements – water, earth, fire and air – are transmitted in such a way that the viewer is drawn into and becomes deeply immersed in the ensorcelled Tarkovskian environment with the totality of all senses; the images of preternatural elements on the screen are intensely tactile, fully alive in their fluctuating states. The Time is also tactile; in Slavoj Žižek's words (2014), for Tarkovsky, 'time is not just neutral, light medium within which things just happen; we feel the density of time itself.' In *Nomos alpha*, the structural layers of the two Paths are articulated by the textural morphologies that oscillate between the two poles of densities: the states of solidity and liquidity, in Deluzian terms, striated – expressed by the various percussive techniques (col legno, battuto, pizzicato, etc.) and smooth – expressed by the extended glissandi and sustained tone; these two states collide through the combinatorial techniques. The glissandi in *Nomos alpha* are as tactile as the Tarkovskian glissandi-images: the long glistening roots slowly pulled from the ground, undulating grass, arborescent silhouettes and ubiquitary manifestations of water. The opposing forces of fire and water, occurring simultaneously in a coagulum of time and space, collide – in the two Paths of *Nomos alpha* the combinatorial techniques embody the intensity of such confrontation. Tarkovsky's tunnels are another example of cinematographic 'glissandi': in *Solaris* (1972) the protagonists are trapped inside the spaceship's endless interior 'tunnel' – a spatial configuration in which the only way to move forward is to travel inwards, into the abyss of their own consciousness. Another example of an extended smooth glissando-tunnel is embodied in the image of the vehicle passing through the series of underpasses in the perpetual movement along the anonymous highway, as if frozen in the moment. In *Stalker*, the 'meat grinder' scene depicts the Scientist's slow vacillating motion along the striated 'intestines' of the glissando-tunnel – an uncanny site soaked in water oozing through the walls – towards the mysterious door, which can only be reached by crossing over a basin of polluted water. The archetypal images of the Door and the Threshold are abundant in Tarkovsky's films. Stephanie Buck (2004) asserts the symbolic meaning of a threshold in a Jungian sense, as a place (moment) of a transition from one (tangible) space to another, or from one (psychic) state to another, as an *event* and as a *process*:

> "Threshold is the in-between zone where passage from one sphere or one way of being to another is made possible. [...] At its essence, threshold is the stable center that mediates between and holds the tension of the opposites; it is a place of possibilities where both sides have the potential to be seen and where energy has the opportunity to flow in either direction."

In *Nomos alpha* the two Paths are (dis)connected by the 'thresholds' – the transitions that are either seamless (concealed) or disrupted (visible, singularised by the act of detuning). The first type, therefore, should be played without a break, transiting smoothly from one state (place) to another,[8] in the second type, the act of transition involves an effort of 'crossing over' as a symbolic gesture of a radical tuning down the C string – the 'soul' of the Xenakian cello –as if plunging into the abyss.

Stalker stimulated a multitude of interpretations. For example, the story might be understood as an inner journey, a dream, when the two temporal entities – dream within 'reality' and reality within a 'dream' fold into each other in the protagonists' quest for a mystical *Room* hidden in the labyrinthine abysses of the *Zone*. Tarkovsky creates the interpretative space, in which the 'meaning' eludes an intellectual enquiry alone, as the mystery of existence is the core of his work, which is, essentially, unattainable. In his interview with the cinematographer, Aldo Tassone (1980, 61) probes this issue:

> "*Q: How do you see the Zone? As an imaginary place?*"

Tarkovsky's answer opens the door to the multitude of interpretations and questions.

> "*T: I don't know. In a way, it's a product of the Stalker's imagination. We thought about it this way: he was the one who created that place. [...] I entirely accept the idea that this world was created by the Stalker in order to instil faith—faith in his reality.*"

However, whether Stalker's world, the *Zone*, resides in the Stalker's imagination – his mind and his heart – or occupies a specific physical place, the effort involved in the search for the *Room*, which is the ultimate *reality*, is immense. The physical aspect of performing *Nomos alpha* could also be framed within the dichotomy of the real effort of performing and an effortless 'dreamlike' progression through the soundscapes of Xenakis's 'Zone', transcending physicality of playing through the *intent*.[9] The two Paths might be understood as the expressions of Reality (Path One) and the Dream/the

---

[8] Example of smooth transition: from bar 233 (battuto bow *fcl* – Xenakis clarifies this instruction in the score: '*frapper avec le bois de l'archet*'), to bar 234 (con sordino, *ppp*). The rapid change from the fast, striking movements of the bow to complete stillness requires a high degree of control.

[9] Here, the 'dreamlike' state refers to a particular stage of mastery, when the two elements –'technique' and 'expression' – that may initially, be in the state of a conflict, fuse into a transcendental moment outside the time-space matrix, creating the conditions where the piece 'plays itself'. This is a rare performance experience of immediate 'revelation', described by the performers as 'being in the Zone'.

Zone (Path Two). In *Stalker* the 'reality' is monochrome and the 'dream' (Zone) is shown in luminous hues; the division between the two states/spaces is fluid, ambiguous.[10] However, the Zone is the space where the Real is the only 'reality' and must be faced.

Conclusion: Performing *Nomos alpha* as a 'project'

"I believe that one moves an audience only through rhythm, concentration, and unity."
Robert Bresson (Samuels 1972, 68)

Gérard Pape (2002, 19) elucidates the fundamental nature of Xenakis's expression, the composer who 'forces us to return to the beginning':

> *"Xenakis's music of the Real hides behind no nostalgic concepts of longing for the lost beauty of the past. Xenakis's music is not afraid to touch on the Real of a Universe that is for him both overwhelming in its blind forces of power and intensity and totally indifferent in its cosmic cruelty towards humankind, a mere speck of dust in the infinite [...]."*

For Tarkovsky, the filmmaking was a persistent enquiry into the mystery of life and death – faith, memories and continuity of existence – through a singular style of artistic expression, in a precise, uncompromising manner; his statement 'Emotion is the enemy of spirituality' (2006, 85) conveys his aversion to the individualistic, affected styles of acting and directing. Xenakis expresses his view on the performance of his music that resonates with Tarkovsky's belief:

> *"It's important that the performer should be able to maintain a certain distance from his repertoire."* (Varga 1996, 107)

In this regard, the cinematographic concepts of the French director Robert Bresson, whose work Tarkovsky deeply admired, stimulate associations with the domain of acting methods that relate (in most cases, indirectly) to the musical performance practice. Susan Sontag (1994) explicates the principal motif of Bressonian cinematography as an exploration of the human soul in its instinctive pursuit of liberation through the commitment to a 'project':

---

[10] The Stalker's 'dream scene', with its images, pace and colour, is a meditation on the notions of 'reality' and the 'real', 'reality' and a 'dream' – their interrelations, collusion and transitory nature.

"The true fight against oneself is against one's heaviness, one's gravity. And the instrument of this fight is the idea of work, a project, a task." (Sontag 1994,189)

Project, in this sense, is a process of a consistent, intensely focused research that includes arduous physical training, directed towards a realisation of a fuller artistic identity, unbounded by 'the gravity' of the self. Sontag illuminates the concept of a 'project' and its significance in Bresson's work:

"*the spiritual style of Bresson's heroes is one variety or other of unself-consciousness. (Hence the role of the project in Bresson's films: it absorbs the energies that would otherwise be spent on the self. [...]). Consciousness of self is the 'gravity' that burdens the spirit; the surpassing of the consciousness of self is 'grace' [...].*" (Sontag 1994,193)

Both Tarkovsky and Xenakis were searching for a rigorous artistic expression of the universal laws that underline cosmic existence, through the power of the images, light, movement and sound. The concept of *precision* in their artistic expression is central to both masters. The Xenakis performer is also taking part in this project – the endeavour that comprises all the necessary aspects of performance, where precision means neither a mechanical accuracy, nor an individualistic 'interpretation' of a rhetorical nature. However, the more precise the technical (textual) realisation of the piece, the more music speaks to the listener; at the same time, the technical rigour is a part of a global concept, that of the *intent* with a particular quality of *honest virtuosity*.

For the performer of *Nomos alpha* the question of interpretation takes a significance of a philosophical search that develops and expands during the process of mastering the work, when, initially, a detailed study involves a slow dissections of the each event's 'anatomy' (as it would be for any meta-complex contemporary composition), but at the later stages acquires a different quality and direction – moving from the intellectual and practical issues towards the domains of the intuitive, intensely visceral and profoundly personal. At that moment, the process reveals its principal source of motivational power (intent) that, in the Tarkovskian/Bressonian sense, becomes manifest as a *project* – an ultimate quest, in which the 'Xenakian cello' is both a material tool and a concept.

Bibliography

Bois, Mario. 1980. *Iannis Xenakis, the Man and His Music: A Conversation with the Composer and a Description of His Works*. Westport, Conn: Greenwood Press.

Buck, Stephanie. 2004. "Home, Hearth, and Grave: The Archetypal Symbol of Threshold On the Road to Self." *The Jungian Society for Scholarly Studies Conference, Salve Regina College, Newport, RI*. http://jungiansociety.org/index.php/home-hearth-and-grave-the-archetypal-symbol-of-threshold-on-the-road-to-self (Accessed 15 May 2018).

Chen, Ying-Hsueh. 2017. *Connecting the raw and the abstract (interview)*. [Blog] http://passiveaggressive.dk/ying-hsueh-chen-connecting-the-raw-and-the-abstract–interview/ (Accessed 12 June 2017).

DeLio, Thomas. 1980. "Iannis Xenakis' 'Nomos alpha': The Dialectics of Structure and Materials." *Journal of Music Theory* 24 (1): 63-95.

DeLio, Thomas. 2001. "Xenakis." *Perspectives of New Music* 39 (1): 231-243.

Ferneyhough, Brian. 1995. *Collected Writings*, edited by James Boros and Richard Toop, Amsterdam: Harwood Academic Publishers.

Gualdo, Sylvio. 2010. "On Psappha and Persephassa." In *Performing Xenakis*, edited by Sharon Kanach. Hillsdale, New York: Pendragon Press, 159-166.

Le Guin, Elisabeth. 2006. *Boccherini's Body: An Essay in Carnal Musicology*. Berkeley: University of California Press.

Matossian, Nouritza. 1986. *Xenakis*. New York: Taplinger Publishing; 2005. *Xenakis*. Lefkosia: Moufflon Publications.

Pape, Gérard. 2002. "Iannis Xenakis and the 'Real' of Musical Composition." *Computer Music Journal*, 26 (1): 16-21.

Peck, Robert W. 2003. "Toward an Interpretation of Xenakis's '*Nomos Alpha*.'" *Perspectives of New Music* 41(1): 66-118.

Pleeth, William. 1992. *Cello*. London: Kahn & Averill.

Rink, Jonh. 2003. "In respect of performance: the view from musicology." *Psychology of Music*, 31(3): 303-323.

Samuels, Charles Thomas. 1972. *Encountering Directors*. New York: G. P. Putnam's Sons.

Sontag, Susan. 1994. *Against Interpretation*. London: Vintage.

Strauch, Peter. 2011. In "It's time for Xenakis." 2011. ISSUU, Durand, Salabert, Eschig, https://issuu.com/durand.salabert.eschig/docs/xenakis_english (Accessed 15 March 2018).

Tassone, Aldo. 1980. 'Interview with Andrei Tarkovsky (on *Stalker*)'. In *Andrei Tarkovsky, Interviews*. 2006, edited by John Gianvito, 55-62. Jackson: University Press of Mississippi.

Terraza, Wilfriedo. 2010. "Xenakis' Wind Glissandi Writing." In *Performing Xenakis*, edited by Sharon Kanach. Hillsdale, New York: Pendragon Press, 25-52.

Varga, Bálint András. 1996. *Conversations with Iannis Xenakis*. London: Faber and Faber.

Xenakis, Iannis. 1967. *Nomos alpha*. Boosey and Hawkes.

Xenakis, Iannis, Brown, Roberta and Rahn, John. 1987. "Xenakis on Xenakis." *Perspectives of New Music* 25 (1/2): 16-63.

Video recordings

Reinecke, Franck. 2006. Interview. In *Musica Viva 7 - Iannis Xenakis: Mythos und Technik.* 2006. WERGO, DVD, B.O.A. Videofilmkunst, Munchen.

Slavoj Žižek on Tarkovsky's Stalker from *The Perverts Guide to Cinema.* 2006. Online. https://youtu.be/uWP3N1Oe9ts (Accessed 11 May, 2017).

Filmography

Bresson, Robert. 1956. *Un condamné à mort s'est échappé.* Gaumont, Nouvelles Éditions de films, France.

Tarkovsky, Andrei. 1972. *Solaris.* Mosfilm, Chetvertoe Tvorcheskoe Obedinenie, Soviet Union.

Tarkovsky, Andrei. 1979. *Stalker.* Mosfilm, Vtoroe Tvorcheskoe Obedinenie, Soviet Union.

Chapter 7

Nomos alpha. Remarks on performance

Makis Solomos

Introduction: chthonic vs cosmic performance

Nomos alpha (1965-66) is one of Xenakis's most 'formalised' pieces. Dating from the time of his research on 'outside-time' structures, the piece is calculated down to the last detail, as we can see in the composer's own analysis in his article 'Towards a philosophy of music', of which there are several versions.[1] This is no doubt why his compositional processes have been the subject of several different analyses by musicologists, some of which are very thorough.[2] For the critic Antoine Goléa, *Nomos alpha* was 'the ugliest thing he had ever heard' (in Xenakis 1988, 136).

What a distance we've come since its premiere by Siegfried Palm in Bremen in May 1966! Today, it is greeted with loud applause each time it is performed. However, the piece remains 'difficult' for the listener: it is submerged in the torrent of 144 micro-events, an extreme fragmentation accentuated by the presence of many minutes of silence and tempered only by a few fuller gestures. Its immediate success is no doubt due to its particularly virtuoso instrumental writing, which means that each performance establishes a particular relationship between the musician on stage and his/her audience. A 'unique and integral work in the cello repertoire' (Meunier 1981, 254-255), *Nomos alpha* was (after *Herma*) the second manifestation of virtuosity Xenakis would put before players. As a result, they shied from it 'for many years until a younger generation of cellists took up the challenge' (Matossian 1981, 226). If it has not yet been fully incorporated into the contemporary

---

[1] There are four versions of this article: Xenakis 1966, Xenakis 1968, Xenakis 1971a and Xenakis 1971b / 1992; only the last three include the part concerning *Nomos alpha*.
[2] The most in-depth analyses are: Vandenbogaerde 1968, Delio 1980, Vriend 1981, Cubillas 1993, Solomos 1993, Solomos 1997, Schaub 2014. The other analyses are: Naud 1975, Matossian 1981 (222-244, 226-237), Landy 1991, Lai 2001, Jones 2002, Agon et al 2004.

cello repertoire, this is because it remains particularly difficult to play – but more and more musicians are now taking it on.

This article will focus on the performance of the piece, a subject, which has still been little investigated (see Meunier 1981, Monighetti 1981, Peck 2003, Uitti 2010, Nakipbekova forthcoming). We can divide the musicians having taken up the challenge into three generations. The first includes Palm, who recorded it in 1974 (Palm 1975) and Pierre Penassou who was the first to perform *Nomos alpha* in France and had already recorded it in 1968 (Penassou 1968). We could also place Rohan de Saram in the same generation, with a certain lag (see his recording: Saram 1992). Saram had the opportunity of playing the piece several times in front of Xenakis, who, as we know, gave very limited instructions to players. In the second generation we might place Pierre Strauch (1992), the cellist of the Ensemble InterContemporain French cellist Christophe Roy and the Belgian Arne Deforce. Finally, there is no shortage of names when it comes to the third generation: Martina Schucan, Moritz Müllenbach (Roy's pupil) and Alfia Nakipbekova to name but three.

Here, I would like to compare the recorded versions made by Christophe Roy and Arne Deforce, sometimes making reference to a few other recordings, in order to illustrate certain points. Interviews carried out with our two main musicians will sometimes be quoted from.

Born in 1960, Christophe Roy, a contemporary music specialist and co-founder of the Aleph ensemble and the Nomos ensemble, worked at length on the piece before performing it in a concert setting – note that beforehand he played *Charisma*, an equally difficult but less virtuoso piece for cello and clarinet.[3] During his first meeting with Xenakis he asked him few questions [4] but found beneficial Xenakis's remarks on the 'poetry of harmonics', in which he requested that the grain, the substance of the sound be made audible rather than the sinusoidal sound. He recorded it in 1998. Born in 1962, Arne Deforce did not meet Xenakis. In his interview, he insists that he produced an

---

[3] "*From Xenakis, I started by working on Charisma, with Dominique Clément, a piece that allowed me to enter Xenakis' universe head on. We sweated on this work, which lasts 4 minutes and in which there are only twenty sounds to play, for a whole year before getting what we wanted! This was in 1975, shortly after the composition of the piece, at a time when we were very young, still students... Throughout this time, for several years, I kept Nomos alpha on a stand - I was doing a lot other stuff in parallel.*" (Christophe Roy).

[4] "*I was twenty-five years old at the time and I was very intimidated. I have not had a real discussion with Xenakis as perhaps Siegfried Palm or others had had before.*" (Christophe Roy).

intuitive version of the piece, without, for example, using a metronome.[5] He adds that he 'sings' it from beginning to end (as with other pieces he plays) and he compares it to the research on multiple vocal and theatrical articulations in Berio's *Sequenza III*.[6] Coming in 2011, it was part of a complete collected recording of Xenakis's cello pieces (Deforce 2011).

Deforce likes to refer to Gilles Deleuze. The following quote from the French philosopher appears on his CD cover:

> "In order for music to free itself, it will have to pass over to the other side – there where territories tremble, where the structures collapse, where the echoes get mixed up, where a powerful song of the earth is unleashed, the great ritornello that transmutes all the airs it carries away and makes return." (In Deforce 2011, 13)

As we will see later, Deleuze emphasises the *cosmic* character of modernity, which is something that could be attributed to Deforce's recording. We could say that Christophe Roy's version, however, comes from the bottom of the earth, that it is somehow *Chthonian*.

Tempos, difficulties, getting inside the sound, final section

Tempos, difficulties, getting inside the sound

To start with, an easy comparison: the overall length of each recording. Here, Roy and Deforce have something in common: they give us long versions, 18'50" and 19'05" respectively. The Palm version only lasts 14'39" and Saram's is only 15'20". On initial analysis, our first-generation players are right to produce short versions.[7] In the score, Xenakis specifies the piece as lasting about 15'. As the tempo (and therefore the overall duration of the piece) is one

---

[5] "*When I did this version, I did it purely artistically, even intuitively, obviously respecting the score; for example, I never worked with metronomes when I recorded - at first I did, of course, yes.*" (Arne Deforce).

[6] "*I have a fairly "vocal" approach to contemporary cello. In Nomos Alpha, for example, I can sing the piece from beginning to end. I do this for many pieces I play. It's a way of giving body to the music for me, even the most abstract or noisy sequences. It's a way of playing this music more in an organic rather than an analytical way. So ...* [he hums the beginning of the piece], *it's almost like Sequenza III by Berio. I try to internalise everything corporally and vocally. I see Nomos alpha as an abstract song contained within the cello's multiple voices.*" (Arne Deforce).

[7] Note that Strauch's version is even shorter: 12'40".

of the formalised parameters of *Nomos alpha* (it has three values, whose alternations follow the rotations of a group consisting of a triangle), it ought to be followed. But the task is impossible, for the two reasons that will be set out below. Xenakis himself was probably fully aware of this impossibility. Indeed, when we calculate how long the piece should last, we end up with 10' 26"![8] One might suppose that he specifies 15' to account for the time taken with the scordatura that takes place during the piece (in four passages, including the final passage, the bass string must be tuned very low, which means therefore that it needs to be re-tuned three times). However, far less time is needed for the scordatura than the additional 4'34". Unless one assumes a miscalculation, then, it might be hypothesised that the inclusion of this additional period of time was Xenakis's way of taking the utopian nature of his requirements into account.

Utopian nature: the first reason why the second generation of performers takes longer to play *Nomos alpha* is obvious. They try to play *everything* or at least play as much as possible, the piece being of an extreme virtuosity. As Deforce explains, in the Palm and Saram versions, many details are lost and, as a result, tension is also lowered.[9] Roy emphasises the fact that Xenakis considers the cello as a set of possibilities that tend towards the infinite (which is also where the idea of the low scordatura comes in).[10] He adds that everything is playable, that is to say, in the temporality of the written score that we can only move towards by playing the piece more slowly. A typical example is the pizzicato from the very beginning (see Example 7. 1). The string is supposed to be plucked 20 times within 2". Saram plays slightly faster, but he only plucks 10 times. Roy does pluck 20 times, but to do this, he is forced to take 3.5". Note that Deforce makes this passage last as long as Roy,

---

[8] The piece contains: a) 188 bars at 4/4 with a tempo minim = 75 MM; b) 93 bars at 4/4 with a tempo minim = 84 MM; c) 9 bars at 4/4 with a tempo minim = 62 MM; d) a few incomplete measurements totalling 3'5".

[9] "*In Siegfried Palm's version, and also in Rohan de Saram's – these are the first versions – sometimes I tend to lose some tension [because of the rapid tempo that stops you from playing everything]. In Nomos alpha, I take certain liberties regarding the formalised aspects of the composition and I approach the question of tempo as a way of taking time to get inside the sound, to bring out the sound event, so that we can capture the energetic sensations of sound: to 'make audible' as Deleuze said.*" (Arne Deforce).

[10] "*You see immediately that Xenakis has a vision of the cello as a set of gigantic notes, in a space that tends towards infinity.*" (Christophe Roy).

but plucks twice as many times. This is because, having been a guitarist, he kept a long fingernail on his thumb, which he uses as a plectrum.[11]

Example 7.1: *Nomos alpha*: bars 1-2

© Copyright 1967 by Boosey & Hawkes Music Publishers Ltd. Reproduced by permission of Boosey & Hawkes Music Publishers Ltd.

The second reason for the slower tempo adopted by Roy and Deforce stems from an apparent paradox: the piece is made up of micro-events (except for the slower 'path 2' sequences), but it must nevertheless be possible to *get inside the sound*. Our two musicians agree on this point.[12] Getting inside the sound: although, on paper, a piece composed of notes and parametric in its conception, *Nomos alpha* is, like any other work by Xenakis, a *music-of-sound* – a piece of *composed sound*, to be precise (see Solomos 2013, 352-361). However, whether *composed* (Xenakis) or *exposed* (Cage or Scelsi), sound needs time, both physically and mentally, and as much for the listener as for the performer. In *Nomos alpha*, beats, which are a literal way of 'entering the sound', are characteristic of this. The 'beats', Xenakis instructs the musician, are achieved by: 'slightly raising or lowering (respectively) the note thus marked so that it 'beats' against the second note, at a rhythm indicated by the figure, which expresses beats per second' (Xenakis 1967b). For Example 7. 2, Saram manages to play much of what is written, but as he plays in the tempo of the score and even a little faster (3" instead of 3.5"), the ear struggles to follow. Roy and

---

[11] *"At the time when I played the guitar, I had the classical guitarist's nail, which I kept, and which works a little like a plectrum. This gives a tremolo-pizzicato that I love. It's a technique I've developed, and that I've used with other composers such as Richard Barrett, Raphael Cendo and Hèctor Parra."* (Arne Deforce).

[12] *"I have to divide up the tempo proposed by Xenakis in a major way, which makes it possible to get into the sound in a more in-depth way - I think it's Flaubert who said: if we want to find something beautiful, we need to look at it for a long time!* [laughs]" Christophe Roy. *"In some places, I would like to take some time to bring in effects that are written and prescribed in the score. For example, the beat effect. If you do it in the given tempo, sometimes you can't bring in these beats, or give them to the ear either."* (Arne Deforce).

Deforce play the passage much more slowly (6" and 7.5" respectively), thus allowing the listener to enter more deeply into the vibration.

Example 7.2: *Nomos alpha*: page 1, system 3, bars 5-7

© Copyright 1967 by Boosey & Hawkes Music Publishers Ltd. Reproduced by permission of Boosey & Hawkes Music Publishers Ltd.

To conclude on tempo and the overall lengths of recordings, we note a difference between our two musicians. Roy tends to respect the proportions; he slows down in a uniform way. Deforce, however, slows down certain events so as to enlarge the spectrum and to make audible certain energetic dimensions of the piece.[13]

The final section

Special mention needs to be made of the last section of the piece. The final sequence of *Nomos alpha*, bars 365-386 (Example 7. 3), conclude both path 2 and the entire work. As a result, they are treated as a composition in the composition, in the manner of the final 'tourniquet' (Batigne 1981, 181) in *Persephassa*. Thus they are not governed by any possible systematisation of path 2 and constitute a supreme gesture of compositional freedom. This is perhaps why such extreme virtuosity is solicited.

---

[13] *"A very special case in the piece, where I take a lot of time, comes in the three sections where sensational sounds are created with the bass string in scordatura."* (Arne Deforce).

Nomos alpha. Remarks on performance

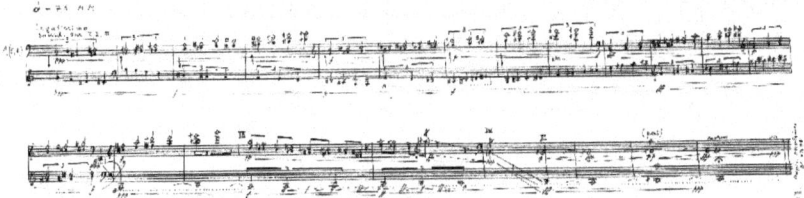

Example 7.3: *Nomos alpha*: **final section of the piece**

© Copyright 1967 by Boosey & Hawkes Music Publishers Ltd. Reproduced by permission of Boosey & Hawkes Music Publishers Ltd.

In this passage, there's a scale of 96 pitches spread over 8.5 octaves, consisting of three movements: a whole tone scale ascending or descending; a three-quarter tone scale ascending or descending; a one and one quarter tone scale ascending only. The development is very complex result, as shown in the graph for Example 7. 4. Moreover, another complex development is superimposed over this one of pitches; that of intensities (Example 7. 5). It is absolutely impossible to play what is written. Some performers use a second cellist, hidden behind the scenes. Others pre-record a part, either at the performance or during the recording: this is so for Deforce.[14] To my knowledge, Roy is one of the few to play it as it is, using a very particular harmonic technique.[15] The result is striking: besides the significant slowing down and the transformation of the timbre, this

---

[14] *"How to play the final section depends on the type of concert (with or without electronics). I can play with a pre-recorded tape, in mono and with a speaker half-hidden behind my chair, creating a deus ex machina effect, bearing in mind that the passage ends very quickly before the audience realises what is really happening. There is a certain Greek theatre heroism, if you will, in hearing and seeing someone play the impossible. Several times after a concert people have come up to me to ask how I was able to play these two lines at the same time. Where the pre-recorded option isn't available, I try to survive by exhausting the possible in what is written. It's horrendous, but wonderful at the same time."* (Arne Deforce).

[15] *"In this passage, the notation is incomplete. It is impossible to play the harmonics of a fourth written with a note held simultaneously. Beyond a few of the sounds, the fingering requested by Xenakis cannot be done. This implies that everyone does their own version. [...] The solution that I adopted is to replace the harmonics of a fourth by harmonics of an octave, fifth, fourth, third major and third minor, so that a gesture can be obtained that descends visually on the string and ascends for the ear. This has a magical side: we see the hand going down and we hear a sound going up! [...] We thus manage to do enough to make the idea clear and perceptible. This pre-supposes a rather slow tempo to really control things and give this liquid aspect."* (Christophe Roy).

technique produces a rather peculiar fragility, which contrasts with the energetic power of the other parts of the piece.

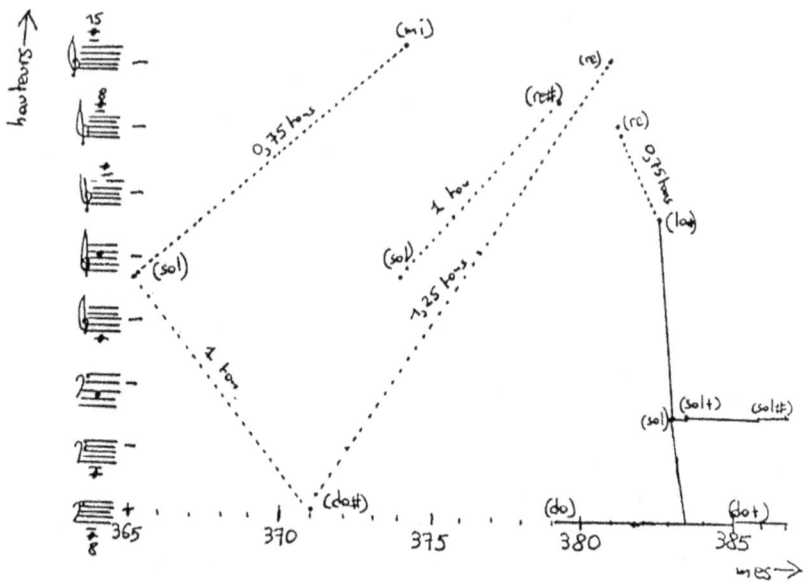

Example 7.4: *Nomos alpha*: graph of the pitches in the final section
(realised by the author)

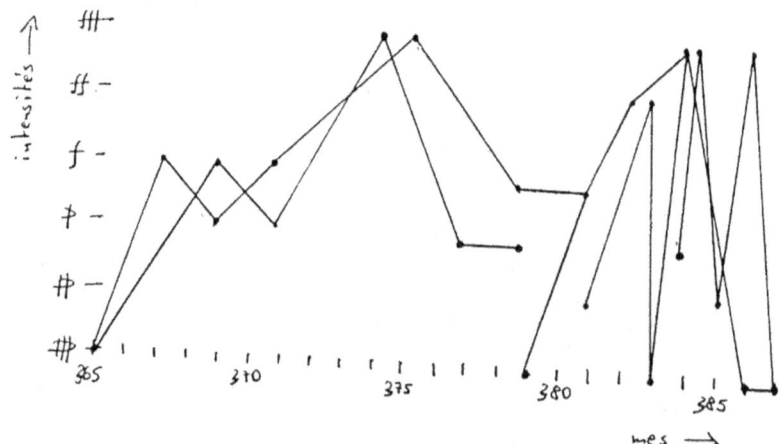

Example 7.5: *Nomos alpha*: graph of the intensities in the final section
(realised by the author)

Specifically Xenakian aspects: sound, energy, gestuality

Let us now turn to some specifically Xenakian aspects, including the question of sound, which has just been mentioned. For Roy, sound and sonority are fundamental elements when he plays Xenakis.[16] His way of playing accentuates the ruggedness that characterises the Xenakis sound, a perfectly controlled ruggedness, in which each detail finds its place. This aspect is, of course, related to the other very Xenakian characteristic that Roy accentuates with particular enthusiasm: energy. Finally, energy is related to the third very Xenakian element: the gesture – energy is linked to the body in its totality, it is gestural. It is as if everything came from 'down below', from the ground – hence the term 'chthonian' – giving the sound the power of a tree with deep roots. In the last section, however, Roy brings out the fragility we have mentioned, as if all the energy accumulated had evaporated into thin air. For Deforce, sound is also a decisive element, but apprehended differently. Even if stemming from gesture, it somehow presents itself as autonomous. This undoubtedly comes about because the energy applied is 'cosmic', as analysed by Deleuze:

> *"If there is a modern age, it is, of course, the age of the cosmic. [...] The forces to be captured are no longer those of the earth, which still constitute a great expressive Form, but the forces of an immaterial, nonformal, and energetic Cosmos. [...] This is the postromantic turning point: the essential thing is no longer forms and matters, or themes, but forces, densities, intensities."* (Deleuze and Guattari 1987, 341-342)[17]

This may be why the result is less harsh than in Roy – you might even say there are 'beautiful' sounds in Deforce's interpretation. However, this is not to say that the energy invested by the Belgian musician is abstract. It is just as physical.[18] To search, to elaborate, to sculpt the sound till the point that its

---

[16] *"When I first heard Pierre Penassou playing Nomos alpha in Royan – I was very young, I had not started the cello yet – what struck me very intensely was the sound, which was something I had never heard before or even experienced. I say 'experienced' because I was 1.5 meters away from him, just under a platform. [...] For me, the most important thing in Xenakis is the energetic power, the spell of the sound."* (Christophe Roy).

[17] Copyright 1987 by the University of Minnesota Press. Originally published as *Mille Plateaux*, volume 2 of *Capitalisme et Schizophrénie* ©1980 by Les Editions de Minuit, Paris, and The Athlone Press. Used by permission of Bloomsbury Publishing Plc.

[18] *"For me, the energy comes very naturally. It's very corporal. I tend to play contemporary music in a very physical way. This energetic aspect is a kind of commitment where everything comes together in a 'sound-becoming': the mind, the body, the gesture, the mental or the emotional, the psychic and the physical."* (Arne Deforce).

energy becomes an authentic sensorial experience, such is the goal. This difference between our two musicians is accentuated in the recording. Deforce gives us a very elaborate result: almost an electroacoustic work. This reinforces the autonomous nature of the sound, as if it had no cause. Hence, perhaps, the tendency towards a 'beautiful' sound.[19] The Belgian cellist indicates that he carried out extensive editing, sometimes going as far as to edit isolated notes. For him, the result given by the recording is an end in itself, an autonomous work of art, that one apprehends for itself, independently of live performance.[20] It is not insignificant that he appreciates the electroacoustic music of Xenakis and he believes that players of Xenakis's work should be inspired by it.[21] In Roy, the recording is less sophisticated. It is conceived as an image of the performance. The cellist explains that Joël Perrot, the sound engineer, was interested in the living energy and the continuity, wanting to capture the singular character of the moment of performance. However there has been some editing on the long passages – and, of course, the moments of scordatura are cut.

Some other aspects

Pitch

The question of pitch is always delicate in this builder of sound that is Xenakis. At the time of the composition of *Nomos alpha*, he attached great importance to it. As has been mentioned, this was the time of his research on

---

[19] "Another dimension of the 'beautiful' that helped me greatly in approaching the problem of the virtuosity of Nomos alpha comes from meditations on the concept of athletics of the ancient Greeks (I'm thinking, for example, of the famous bronze statues like the Poseidon of the Temple of Artemis at Ephesus). This led me to develop a very refined and elaborate muscular technique, accentuating victory over matter that gives glory to the corporal and beauty to the cello sound body." (Arne Deforce).

[20] "The recording took me three hours. We did five versions of the piece, in large parts: the first three pages, then two more pages, and so on. Afterwards, we worked and edited, sometimes even taking better notes from a different version. For me, you don't record a CD in the image of a concert. Rather it's about offering something distinct. As Glenn Gould said, a recording is a work of art in itself." (Arne Deforce).

[21] "I love Xenakis's electronic music. If I gave a class to a cellist who wanted to play Nomos alpha, I would tell him that you not only have to listen to the orchestral works, but also the electronic works. It's a matter of immersing yourself in electronics and then returning to the cello. The speed with which we play a pizzicato or a Bartók pizzicato can contain something reminiscent of electronic music: a kind of nervousness, as if the fingers and the bow had been electrified while playing this piece." (Arne Deforce).

'outside-time' structures, in which pitch constitutes the best model. After setting out the structures of pitch in Greek antiquity and Byzantine music at length, his article 'Towards a Metamusic' (Xenakis 1967b) introduces the theory of pitch 'sieves' – which is to say, scales. And we know that he spent a lot of time on sieve-construction for *Nomos alpha*. Pitch, then, is a crucial element in *Nomos alpha*. Nevertheless, we are tempted to relativise this aspect. First of all, it is now understood that Xenakis is a musician of sound. This does not mean he was a musician of 'timbre' (in the manner of a certain French tradition), but a composer who put all the 'parameters' of sound at the service of an overall conception of music, synonymous, in this sense, with 'sound': timbre of course, but also space, rhythm and, just as importantly, pitch – these elements can be thought of as serving sound. And it is obvious that the parameter of 'sound complexes' is more important than the pitch sieves in *Nomos alpha*. Next, those who have analysed them know that there are many 'gaps' between the theoretical sieves (those built by Xenakis) and the practical ones (the notes found in the score), differences that come from calculation errors or theoretical errors (see Solomos 1997). For those who the word 'error' frightens, it should be remembered that at the time Xenakis calculated his sieves using constructions on graph paper, which easily generates errors, whether at the time of the construction of the sieve or, more often, during transcription onto staffs, without even going into the errors resulting from the concrete choice of a pitch during the composition of a precise passage using the sieve in question. Moreover, because of the multiplication of parameters calculated separately in *Nomos alpha*, contradictions can often be found. For example, there is also a parameter 'register' specifying that, in such and such a passage, only a particular register should be used. However, it may happen that the sieve used has no pitches in this register. Finally, it may be useful to remember that the *Nomos alpha* sieves are often very complex (their mode of repetition is not the octave) and too little repeated for the listener to memorise them. In short, for the listener, they do not have the same preponderance as the sound complexes. It is, therefore, justified that many performers today play *Nomos alpha* with more attention to sound than pitch. Nevertheless, we must not go too far in this interpretation. Thus, the temptation to treat the quarter-tones in the passage in Example 7. 6 as a *bisbigliando* (a particular timbre) – a temptation to which Strauch (1992) yields, which produces a kind of insect hum - must, it seems to me, be avoided. I think the time has come to reconcile Xenakis the sculptor-of-sound with Xenakis the theorist, who wants to rebuild the pitch cosmos. A passage like the one just quoted has a real *melodic* intention. Such passages, where the melodic intention is obvious, can be found in *Oresteia*, composed during the same period as *Nomos alpha* (see Example 7. 7). Roy's recording is particularly successful on this point: he reaches that delicate compromise between the realm of pitch and the emphasis on sound.[22] As for Deforce, because of the tendency to think of sound as autonomous, he is rather of the school of those who consider pitch as secondary.

Example 7.6: *Nomos alpha*, page 1, system 4, last 2 bars

© Copyright 1967 by Boosey & Hawkes Music Publishers Ltd. Reproduced by permission of Boosey & Hawkes Music Publishers Ltd.

Silence and continuity

A word on the silences. At first, Xenakis probably intended to treat them as a formalised, calculated parameter. In Vandenbogaerde's analysis, which is reproduced in one of the versions of 'Towards a philosophy of music' (Xenakis 1971a, 111-118), mention is made of the fact that the silences are calculated using a kinematic diagram, as is the register parameter. However, Xenakis's own analysis does not mention them, which suggests that being too occupied with the other parameters, he ended up treating the silences in an intuitive way. Whatever the case may be, in *Nomos alpha*, silences play a vital role. They contribute to the extreme fragmentation of the piece.

Roy explains that when he met Xenakis, he seemed somewhat troubled by this fragmentation. This is why he abbreviates the silences within the sections slightly when he plays the piece. He thus tends towards greater continuity, which is reinforced by his tendency to interpret certain pitch passages melodically. However, in his recording, this continuity is contradicted by the fact that little processing is introduced (in particular, no reverberation) and that, consequently, the silences tend to be felt more strongly. Deforce, however, also seems to abbreviate the silences inside the sections slightly.

---

[22] *"Pitch is the fundamental parameter if you want to create timbre: the sound depends directly on the emission of pitches; the sound constitutes the essential element, but it is a result. If we lose sight of this, we get lost in approximation. [Question: We feel the importance of pitch in your version. What strikes us sometimes is that we hear Xenakis marked by Byzantine music in sections with quarter-tones reminiscent of the Oresteïa.] Indeed, in Nomos alpha there are sometimes kinds of tetrachords that sound like modes – 'nomos' also means mode."* (Christophe Roy).

This results, in the recording, in a continuity that is reinforced by the (moderate) use of reverberation. When it comes to the silences between the sections, Roy accentuates them, thus accentuating the separation between the sections.

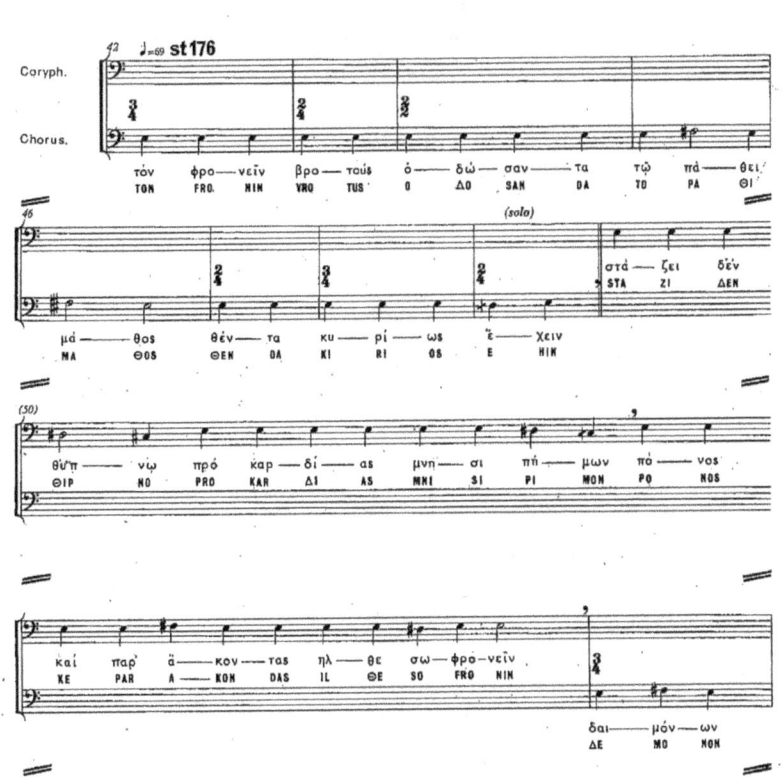

Example 7.7: *Oresteia*, p. 6

© Copyright 1966 by Boosey & Hawkes Music Publishers Ltd. Reproduced by permission of Boosey & Hawkes Music Publishers Ltd.

Relationship to Xenakis's theory

The compositional system and the score

One last question: what relationship do our two musicians have with the theoretical system developed by Xenakis for *Nomos alpha*? In interviewing them, I asked them if they wished to transmit this theoretical system to the listener, and, in particular, the idea that the piece is built on the model of the rotations of a cube, proposing the transfer of a geometrical and spatial model to the sonic and temporal universe of music. Both said they wanted to do this. How to proceed with this transmission remains, of course, a delicate question: Roy mentions the play on dynamics able to create a space sensation, which serve as a figure for the cube rotations. As for Deforce, adopting the Deleuzian language, we could say that he tends towards a 'cube-becoming' when he plays the piece.[23] Both musicians also enlarge the score, which is a reproduction of the composer's manuscript, in order to play more comfortably. But, while Deforce finds it to be very well written and says he likes working with the handwriting of the composer, Roy finds it difficult to read and would like a new edition.

The gaps and errors

As has been mentioned, every Xenakis analyst knows that there are many discrepancies between the composer's calculations and what is found in the score. A certain mythology is in circulation concerning this. In the past, to moderate the image of the composer-mathematician, a cold calculator, and

---

[23] *"When we compare what we play from the score with the 'sound complexes' we are supposed to play, we realise that we did not necessarily guess the type of sound that Xenakis wanted. It's interesting, because it makes us see the sound we're playing in a different way. [...] For example, he talks about 'ionized atoms' for the beats. This enables us to see that, what interests him, is hearing the inner pulsation. The cube rotations, for example, are indicated on the score by letters. We must be aware of this. When I play, I think about this a lot. [...] With the cube, Xenakis has a 3D vision, which must be heard. The whole dynamic of the piece (the nuances) is translated into distance and proximity. For me, it is important to conceive of the pitches vertically (an infinite space in this direction) and then nuances in the other direction: sound exists in a curved space. The cello makes this happen. For example, you can be playing extreme nuances and, at the same time, a limit is reached very quickly. You end up designing a sound sculpture in this space."* (Christophe Roy). *"I was very interested in the analyses of the piece – even if they are too mathematical for me. The concept of cube rotation fascinated me a great deal and inspired me. How to show, thanks to the rotation of the cube, that one effect is linked to another, a tremolo to a pizzicato for example? I would say that you yourself have to become this cube in rotation. Each of my two arms – or the hundred arms in Kottos – becomes a particular bow. This is why I say metaphorically that I don't play with one bow, but with ten. Thanks to this metaphor, I physically integrate the concept of the cube and its rotations to become the multiple voices of the cello with its particular modes of being played, to change from one to the next. I think this is where the real virtuosity of Nomos alpha lies, and especially what Xenakis calls 'the joy of the triumph in exceeding one's own capacities.' The rotation of the cube is conceived of as a prism of transformation."* (Arne Deforce).

Nomos alpha. Remarks on performance 123

especially when he made use of computers for the first time (ST program), it was said that Xenakis

> "keeps what needs to be held kept, changes what he feels should be changed, grafting his own choices (where his taste and sensitivity can be introduced) onto the choice of the machine [...]."

We would conclude that

> "in this method of working every opportunity is given to the personality of the musician to come out." (Barraud 1968, 185)

This is certainly true: Xenakis often makes choices that, in highly formalised works, can blow the theoretical system and its calculations apart. However, it is important to add that, often, the gaps largely come from errors, as we remarked previously regarding the calculation of pitch sieves (errors generated by their transcription on staffs or the choice of pitches in a sieve to compose a passage).

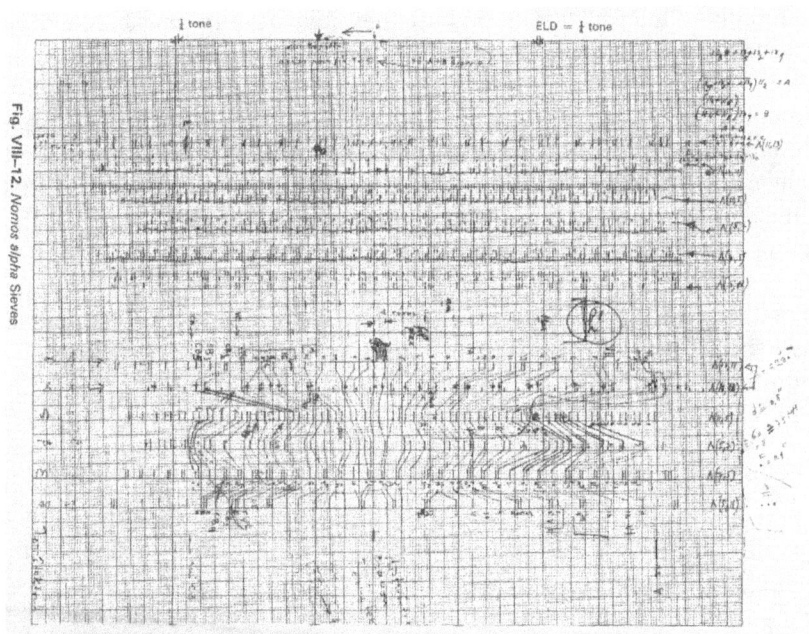

Example 7.8: Xenakis 1992, 234

Xenakis's Archives. Reproduced with permission from Mâkhi Xenakis.

To give an example: a manifest error is highlighted in a manuscript provided by Xenakis in the 1992 edition of *Formalized Music* (see Example 7. 8). The error concerns the construction of sieve Λ (11, 13). The analysis – the comparison between the theoretical sieve and the notes found in the score – shows a gap of more than 50%. Obviously, such a gap does not arise out of choice. As the handwritten annotations of Xenakis in Greek attest, an error was made. On the left, it reads: 'αλλάζει. Γιατί;' (this changes, why?). In fact, Xenakis got it wrong when he wrote one of the sieve modules, shifting it, which, in the final calculation, produces wrong pitches, hence the huge gap. Recognising this error, but unwilling or unable to reconstruct the sieve (the music had probably already been composed and published), he tried to legitimise it by indicating at the top of the manuscript: 'από το μηδέν ισχύει μόνο για τα C. Το A+B έχουν O' (as of zero this only applies to the Cs. The A+Bs are O), an arrow referring this indication to a particular place that is the 'origin' (O) of the module A+B of the sieve. It is obvious that having two origins in a sieve does not make sense!

When I questioned the two cellists about the gaps, they did not seem to be aware of this issue. Maybe, in the future, with the help of a critical edition of the score, musicians might raise it? This does not mean that they should necessarily 'correct' all 'errors' because they are part of the music…There is, however, one particularly obvious error that many musicians have tried to correct. It is located between systems 5 and 6 on page 1 of the score (see Example 7. 9). It reads *D-A*, a perfect fifth that is very explosive in the context of *Nomos alpha*. Palm and Saram play it. Since then, in Roy and in the third generation, musicians have often played a sustained *A*. It is likely that this correction comes from the extract of the score reproduced in one of the versions of 'Towards a philosophy of music' (see Example 7. 10). However, this is not the right correction! In terms of the theoretical sieve, the musician should play sustained *D* with the error rather being a wrong key indication: there should be an *F* at the beginning of system 6 of the score. Deforce is one of the few to play this *D*.[24]

---

[24] *"I always saw the note at the end of the fifth system as a legato note. Also, it seemed clear to me that it was in the wrong key and that it needed to be in F to make the related note logical. Just as the key of C is missing in the third measure of this system."* (Arne Deforce).

Nomos alpha. Remarks on performance

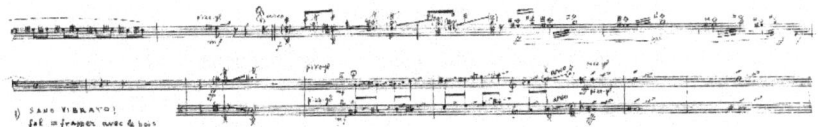

Example 7.9: *Nomos alpha*, page 1, systems 5-6

© Copyright 1967 by Boosey & Hawkes Music Publishers Ltd. Reproduced by permission of Boosey & Hawkes Music Publishers Ltd.

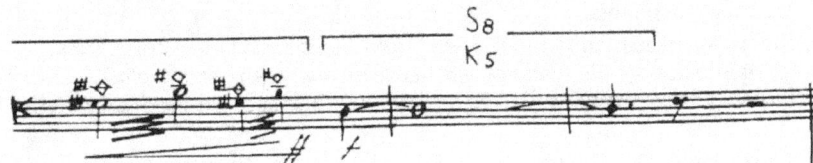

Example 7.10: Xenakis 1971 a, 116

© Copyright 1967 by Boosey & Hawkes Music Publishers Ltd. Reproduced by permission of Boosey & Hawkes Music Publishers Ltd.

To conclude

This article sketches out a preliminary analysis of the performance of *Nomos alpha*, comparing, in particular, two versions, given by two 'second generation' musicians playing Xenakis. The analysis needs to be continued, both to refine the comparison and to introduce other versions as well. To limit ourselves to our two cellists, I would like to add in conclusion – but also in an assertion that should not be taken too seriously – that their respective chthonic and cosmic characters are also revealed in the photos given in Example 7. 11.

Example 7.11: Christophe Roy (left) and Arne Deforce (right)

Translation from the French: Jack Sims.

Bibliography

Interviews with Christophe Roy and Arne Deforce carried out in September 2017.

Agon, Carlos, Andreatta, Moreno, Assayag, Gérard, and Schaub, Stéphan. 2004. "Formal Aspects of Iannis Xenakis 'Symbolic Music': A Computer-Aided Exploration of Compositional Processes." *Journal of New Music Research* 33(2): 145-160.

Barraud, Henri. 1968. *Pour comprendre les musiques d'aujourd'hui.* Paris: Seuil.

Batigne, Jean. 1981. "Sur *Persephassa* et *Pléiades.*" In *Regards sur Iannis Xenakis.* Paris: Stock.

Cubillas, Morales Juan Manuel. 1993. *Iannis Xenakis,* Nomos alpha*: una aproximacion inicial hacia el analisis de un encuentro, en el siglo XX, entre la musica y la matematica (Teoria de Grupos).* PhD diss.: Universidad Catolica (Valparaiso, Chile).

Deleuze, Gilles and Guattari, Félix. 1987. *A Thousand Plateaus,* translated by Brian Massumi. Minneapolis: University of Minnesota Press.

Delio, Thomas. 1980. "I. Xenakis: *Nomos alpha.*" *Journal of Music Theory* 24 (1): 63-96. In *Contigious Lines,* edited by Thomas Delio, 3-30. University Press of America.

Jones, Evan. 2002. "An Acoustic Analysis of Col Legno Articulation in Iannis Xenakis' *Nomos Alpha.*" *Computer Music Journal* 26 (1): 73-86.

Lai, Antonio. 2001. "*Nomos alpha* de Iannis Xenakis. La matrice disciplinaire et une évaluation contextuelle de l'œuvre." In *Présences de Iannis Xenakis,* edited by Makis Solomos, 125-140. Paris: CDMC.

Landy, Leigh. 1991. *What's the Matter with Today's Experimental Music?,* 77-94 and 217-224. Chur: Harwood Academic Publishers.

Matossian, Nouritza. 1981. *Iannis Xenakis,* Paris: Fayard.

Meunier, Alain. 1981. "Sur *Nomos alpha.*" In *Regards sur Iannis Xenakis,* edited by Hugues Gerhards, 254-256. Paris: Stock.

Monighetti, Ivan. 1981. "Sur *Nomos alpha* et *Kottos.*" In *Regards sur Iannis Xenakis,* edited by Hugues Gerhards, 252-253. Paris: Stock.

Nakipbekova, Alfia. Forthcoming. *Performing Contemporary Cello Music: Defining the Interpretative Space. Case Study: Nomos alpha by Iannis Xenakis.* PhD diss.: University of Leeds.

Naud, Gilles.1975. "Aperçus d'une analyse sémiologique de *Nomos alpha.*" *Musique en Jeu* 17: 63-72.

Peck, Robert W. 2003. "Toward an Interpretation of Xenakis's *Nomos Alpha.*" *Perspectives of New Music* 41(1): 66-118.

Schaub, Stéphan. 2014. *Formalisation mathématique, univers compositionnels et interprétation analytique chez Milton Babbitt et Iannis Xenakis.* Étude autour de *Semi-Simple Variations* (1956) pour piano de Milton Babbitt et de *Nomos alpha* (1965-66) pour violoncelle de Iannis Xenakis. PhD diss.: Université Paris IV (France).

Solomos, Makis. 1993. *À propos des premières œuvres (1953-69) de I. Xenakis. Pour une approche historique de l'émergence du phénomène du son.* PhD diss.: Université Paris IV (France).

Solomos, Makis. 1997. "Esquisses pré-compositionnelles et œuvre : les cribles de *Nomos alpha* (Xenakis)." *Les Cahiers du CIREM* 40-41: 141-155.

Solomos, Makis. 2013. *De la musique au son. L'émergence du son dans la musique des XXe-XXIème siècles.* Rennes: Presses Universitaires de Rennes.

Uitti, Frances-Marie. 2010. "Notes on Working with Xenakis." In *Performing Xenakis*, edited by Sharon Kanach, 335-341. Hillsdale, New York: Pendragon Press.

Vandenbogaerde, Fernand. 1968. "Analyse de *Nomos alpha*." *Mathématiques et Sciences Humaines* 24: 35-50.

Vriend, Jan. 1981. "*Nomos alpha*, Analysis and Comments." *Interface* 10: 15-82.

Xenakis, Iannis. 1966. "Zu einer Philosophie der Musik / Towards a philosophy of Music." *Gravesaner Blätter* 29: 23-38/39-52.

Xenakis, Iannis. 1967. *Nomos alpha.* Boosey and Hawkes.

Xenakis, Iannis. 1967b. "Vers une métamusique.", *La Nef* 29: 117-140. In Xenakis, Iannis. 1971. *Musique. Architecture*, 38-70. Tournai: Casterman.

Xenakis, Iannis. 1968. "Vers une philosophie de la musique." *Revue esthétique* 2-3-4: 173-210.

Xenakis, Iannis. 1971a. "Vers une philosophie de la musique." In *Musique. Architecture*, 71-119. Tournai: Casterman.

Xenakis, Iannis. 1971b/1992. "Towards a philosophy of Music". In *Formalized Music*, 201-241. Bloomington: University Press.

Xenakis, Iannis. 1988. "A propos de *Jonchaies*." *Entretemps* 6: 133-137.

Discography

Deforce, Arne. 2011. *Iannis Xenakis. Intégrale de l'œuvre pour violoncelle.* CD. æon AECD 1109.

Palm, Siegfried, and Kontarsky, Aloys. 1975. *Webern, Xenakis, Kagel, Zimmermann, Penderecki, Brown, Yun: Zeitgenössische Cellomusik.* Vinyl. Deutsche Grammophon 2530 562.

Penassou, Pierre. 1968. Recording of *Nomos alpha.* In *Iannis Xenakis – Atrées / Morsima-Amorsima / ST/4 / Nomos Alpha.* Vinyl Angel Records S-36560.

Roy, Christophe. 2000. *Violoncelle (Aperghis, Ballif, Kagel, Xenakis).* CD. Grave GRCD 16.

Saram, Rohan de. 1992. Recording of *Nomos alpha.* In *Iannis Xenakis 1. Chamber Music 1955-1990, Claude Helffer and Arditti string quartet.* CD. Auvidis Montaigne.

Strauch, Pierre. 1992. In *Xenakis: Phlegra, Jalons, Keren, Nomos Alpha, Thallein, Naama, A L'Ile De Gorée, Khoaï & Komboï, Ensemble Intercontemporain.* Erato.

Index

Page numbers shown in bold refer to musical examples, page numbers in italics refer to figures and tables.

A

Adorno, Theodor W. 4, 8, 8n.3, 9n.4, 14, 15, 16, 17
arborescences vii, *22*, 24, *33*, 38, 39, 40, 41, 46, 48, 50
architecture 9, 10, 11, 12, 13, *22*, 23, 80

B

Bresson, Robert 104–105
bricolage *22*, 24, *33*
Brownian motion *22*, 24, *33*

C

Cage, John 7–8, 77, 113
chance 4, 5, 7–9, 12, 14, 15, 16, 96n.6
chaos 8, 9
cluster vii, 24, 38, 40, *41*, 44, 46, 47, 50, 95, 97
continuity 21, 34, 39–40, 94–95, 98, 104, 118, 120–121

D

Darmstadt 16
Deleuze, Gilles 111, 112n.9, 117
Deleuzian language 122
density 37, 38, 40, 42, 44, 45, 47, 49, 50, 54, 56, 94n.5, 97, 102

discontinuity 39, 94, 98

E

electroacoustic
 composition/work viii, 34, 69, 70, 85, 118
 music/musician vn.2, viii, 69, 70, 71, 77, 84, 118

F

Ferneyhough, Brian vn2, 94n.5, 99
fluctuation 37, 47, 97, 99
formalisation 12, *22*, 23, 24, 26, 34, 35
Formalized Music /Musique Formelles 26, 37, 124

G

gesamtkunstwerk 10
Gibson, Bezoît vin.5, vii, viii, 21, 70, 71, 74
glissando 11, *12*, 12, 24, 39, 40, 93, 94, 95, 97, 99, 102
graphic representation viii, 38, 41, 56, 56n.4, *57*, 59, *60*, 61, 62, 63
Greek theatre 101, 115n.14
groups 6, 22, *22*, 23, 28–34, 51, 63
group theory 32, 33

H

Harley, James *22*, 23, 25, 71, 74

I

improvisation 15, 70, 82, 83, 84, 99
inside-time 23, 25, *33*, 34, 53
intensity *22*, 25, 37, 90, 102, 104
interpretation viii, ix, 89, 90–92, 98, 99, 100, 101, 103, 105, 117, 119

M

mathematics vi, 15, 21, 26, 34, 35, 10, 26, 33, 101
Matossian, Nouritza *22*, 23, 91, 96, 109
Messiaen 28
modulor 11, 13, 16
montage 21, 82

N

notation 24, 56, 57, 65, 94n.5, 99, 115n.15

O

outside-time vii, 22, 23, 25, 26, 33, 34, 57, 109, 119

P

performance vi, viii, ix, 38n.2, 65, 70, 71, *72*, 82, 84, 89–99, 103n.9, 104–105, 109–110, 115, 118, 125
performer v, viii, ix, 9, 63, 64, 65, 84, 85, 89, 91, 91n.2, 92, 94, 94n.5, 95, 96, 99, 100, 100n.7, 101, 103n.9, 104, 105, 112, 113, 115, 119
Philips Pavilion 9, 11, *12*, 77
pitch viii, 24, 25, 26, 28, 29, 37, 38n.2, 39, 40, 41, 42, 42n.5, 43, 46, 47, 48, 50, 53, 54, 55, 56, 59, 61, *61*, 62, 62n.10, 63, 64, 65, 77, 94, 95, 100, 115, *116*, 118–120, 122n.23, 123, 124
pizzicato 39, 91, 97, 102, 112, 113n.11, 118n.21, 122n.23

R

rhythm/rhythmic *22*, 29, 40, 41, 44–46, 50, 97, 100, 104, 113, 119

S

scales 24, 26, 27, 28, 29, 54, 119
Schaeffer, Pierre vii, 38n.1, 42n.5, 47, 69, 77
scordatura 89, 93n.4, 94, 112, 114n.13, 118
self-borrowing 21
serialism 15, 25
sieves 22, *22*, 23, 24, 25, 28–29, 33, *33*, 34, 54, 119, 123
silence 98–100, 109, 120–121
Solomos, Makis vn.1, vi, vin.5, ix, *22*, 23, 24, 39, 83, 84
sonority vii, viii, 21, *22*, 23, 24, 25, 39, 41, 49, 53, 54, 89, 94, 95, 100, 117
sound v, vii, viii, ix, 9, 11, 13, 17, 23, 24, 25, 34, 37–51, 54, 56, *57*, 59n.8, 65, 69, 70, 71, 74, 75, 76, 77, 79–85, 89, 90, 90n.1, 91n.2, 93, 94, 95, 97, 98, 99, 100, 101, 105, 110, 110n.3, 112n.9, 113, 113n.12, 114n.13, 115n.15, 117,

Index

117nn.16 and 18, 118, 118n.19, 119, 120, 120n.22, 122n.23
complexes 119, 122n.23
density 40, 50
event 38, 112n.9
mass vii, 37, 38, 40, 45, 46, 47, 49, 51
material 69, 71, 82, 84, 85
object 47, 77
quality 46, 50, 77
source 69, 85
Stalker viii, 90, 101–104
stochastic 21, *22*, 23, 25, *33*, 34
   approach 25
   composition 23
   distribution viii, 8, 9, 56, 59
   experience 23
   music 8, 15, 21
   passage 34
   process 23
   synthesis *33*
structure vii, viii, 5, 6, 8, 22, 23, 24, 25, 26, 29, 30, 31, 33, 34, 38, 40, *41*, 50, 51,   77, 84, 95, 96, 97, 99, 100, 109, 111, 119
symbolic
   gesture 103
   logic *22*, 23, *33*
   meaning 102
   music 26

T

Tarkovsky, Andrei viii, 90, 101–104, 105
technique
   compositional vii, 21, 69
   extended 82, 94, 94n.5, 95, 102, 115, 116
   instrumental v, viii, 47, 57, 77, 89–90, 91, 93, 94, 94n.5, 95, 102, 103n.9,

113n.11, 116, 115, 118n.19
   recording 82, 95
texture vii, viii, 21, 40–42, 43, 44, 45, 46, 47, 48, 50, 69, 89, 91, 94, 95, 98, 99, 101
timbre vii, 37, 39, 41, 42, 43, 47, 48, 50, 57, 59, 89, 93n.4, 115, 119, 120n.22

V

volume 10, 43, 45, 46, 47, 48
volumetric 10

X

Xenakis, Iannis
   compositions:
   Achorripsis vii, 21, *22*, 23, 53, 56, 57, 59, *60*
   Aïs 22
   Akrata 22, 26, 27, 28
   Analogiques 69
   Atrées 63
   Bohor vii, viii, 69, 70–71, *72*, *73*, 74–75, *76*, 77, *78*, 79–80, 85
   Concret PH 9, 69
   Diamorphoses 69
   Diatope 69, 80, 82, 83
   Duel 21, *22*
   Ergma 22, 25
   Evryali 22, 24, 95
   Gendy 34
   Gmeeoorh vii, 38, 38n.2, 39–40, *41*, 41, 46–47, 50
   Herma vii, viii, *22*, 26–27, 28, 53–65, 109
   Hibiki-Hana-Ma 69
   Hiketides 21
   Horos 22
   Ittidra 25
   Jonchaies 22, 24

Kraanerg 69
La Légende d'Eer viii, 69, 70, 80, *81*, 83, 84
Metastasis vii, 11–12, 15, 21, *22*, 23, 25
Mikka 22, 24
Morsima–Amorsima 63
Mycènae Alpha (Polytope de Mycène) 69
Nomos alpha vii, viii, xi, *22*, 26, 34, 89–91, 92n.3, 93n.4, 94–98, 100–103, 105, 109–116, 117n.16, 118, 118n.19, 118n.21, 119–125
Nomos gamma 34
Oresteia 119, 120n.22, **121**
Persephassa 22, 29, 114
Pithoprakta 15, 21, *22*, 23, 25, 34, 40
Polla ta Dhina 63
Polytopes 12, 69, 82
Polytope de Cluny 7, 10, 12, 69
Polytope de Montreal 69
S.709 34
S*T 10* 70
Synaphaï 22, 24, 65, 94
Tetras 24

Z

zone 102, 103, 103n.9, 104